P9-DUO-902

Treasured Moments

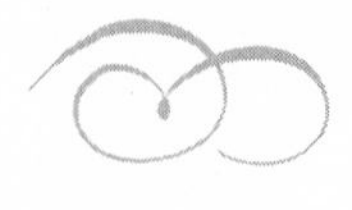

Stories of Love Remembered

Guideposts
COMFORT FROM BEYOND
Series

Treasured Moments

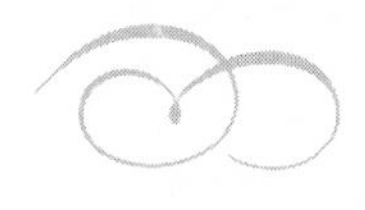

Stories of Love Remembered

Edited by Phyllis Hobe

A Guideposts Book

Acknowledgments

Every attempt has been made to credit the sources of copyrighted material used in this book. If any such acknowledgment has been inadvertently omitted or miscredited, receipt of such information would be appreciated.

All material that originally appeared in Guideposts publications is reprinted with permission. Copyright © 1947, 1964, 1975, 1985, 1990, 1992, 1997, 1998, 1999, 2000, 2001, 2002, 2003, 2004.

Chapter 1 - ALWAYS WITH US
"Together Across the Miles," by Betty R. Graham, "Birthday," by Carolyn Cahill, and "Celebrating Our Dreams," by Kathryn Lay, are used by permission of the authors. "A Letter From Heaven," by A. A., "A Promise Kept," by V. M., and "He Came to Say Good-bye," are used by permission of Dorchester Media. "Clocks Stopping," by Wendy, is from *After-Death Communication,* by Emma Heathcote-James, published by Metro Publishing LTD, 2003; used by permission.

Chapter 2 - UNFORGETTABLE DEVOTION
"Keeping Watch," by Mary M. Alward, and "A Parting Gift," by T. J. Banks, are used by permission of the authors.

Chapter 3 - A SMILE, A TEAR
"She Is Still With Me," by H. M., and "He Came to Say Good-bye," by N. M. Stach, are used by permission of Dorchester Media.

Designed by Jerry O'Brien
Jacket designed by Monica Elias
Cover photo © Digital Vision/Getty Images
Printed in the United States of America

Contents

Introduction

When I was a child, the worst thing about the death of someone I loved was that I would never see that person again. She, or he, was gone, and there was an emptiness in my life.

I was mistaken, and as I grew in years I learned that God has miraculous ways of helping us to deal with our losses.

God gives us memory, which is like a spiritual scrapbook of all the moments we have spent with those we have loved. We feel their closeness, we feel their warmth, and we can share our thoughts with them.

Treasured Moments is a collection of stories by those who have lost loved ones and yet feel their presence. They have been blessed by God's promise that they will one day be reunited with them.

The stories in Chapter 1, *Always With Us,* make us aware that death does not really seperate us from those we loved. A woman who cannot get to her father's funeral service is comforted by memories of his loving ways. A daughter comes across a clock that suddenly starts ticking in her late mother's room.

In Chapter 2, *Unforgettable Devotion,* we read about people who gave beyond their means. A doctor ignored the bills his patients couldn't afford to pay. A wife and mother gives thanks for the grandmother who still guides her life.

In Chapter 3 we meet a woman who can still hear the voice of her twin sister who used to sing in harmony with her when they were young. And a sister, who loved her brother dearly, brings him home to die in the little house that meant so much to him.

The stories in Chapter 4 inspire us to pursue our goals in spite of obstacles. A young girl whose family is destitute is encouraged by her grandmother to stay in school. A young man whose family was destroyed in the holocaust strives to find his own identity.

In Chapter 5 we meet men and women who lives were shaped by people they loved and lost. Kathie Kania remembers the lovable but eccentric Aunt Marge who encourages her to do her best—always. A mother celebrates three of her children who lived not long, but happily.

In all of these true stories we are touched by God's love for us and by the blessing of the memories He has given us of those we have lost. Yes, someday we will be reunited with all those we have loved, but until that time comes we have their spiritual presence in our everyday lives.

PHYLLIS HOBE

CHAPTER

1

Always With Us

For he is our God;
and we are the people of his pasture.
Psalm 95:7, KJV

Together Across the Miles

BETTY R. GRAHAM

When my father died a week before Christmas, I was living in Caracas, Venezuela, with my husband and our two sons. My husband's job with the American Embassy had brought us there. It wasn't our first posting abroad. We'd already lived in Africa and in Central America. My mother had died several years earlier, while we were posted to Honduras. I found it hard to imagine our family without Dad, or Granddad, as the boys called him. I immediately began to make plans to attend the funeral in my hometown of Lansdowne, Maryland.

But since it was so close to Christmas, I soon learned that all the planes to the States had been booked for weeks. There wasn't a seat available on any plane. My spirits sank even deeper than they had when I'd received the news of Dad's death. How could I not be with my sisters and brothers at my own father's funeral?

Then someone from the Embassy told us that it would be possible for me to fly home. The airline was willing to bump a passenger in favor of a seat for me because of the disaster emergency. I began to think what this would mean. If I agreed, then someone who had been looking forward to celebrating Christmas with the living would be disappointed. Besides, if I did go home, it was unlikely that I'd be able to get another plane back in time to celebrate Christmas with my own immediate family. I debated long and hard over the choice.

Mom had died in January six years before, and there wasn't any trouble getting a seat on a plane at that time. And Dad was still alive. He had been so good to Mom during her long, six-year illness. I felt Dad needed all his children to help him through the funeral and his grief. It never even occurred to me not to go.

But this was different. Mom was not there anymore; she wouldn't need my support as Dad had before. My sisters and brothers could manage without me and that unknown passenger, oblivious to the situation, would be able to spend a happy Christmas with those he or she loved. Although it made me sad, I made the decision to stay home and forego my father's funeral.

Since we had come to Caracas, I had been attending a small Baptist mission church. I called the missionary pastor and told him my sad news. He was very comforting. Even though he did not know my father, he suggested that I have a separate memorial service for just my small family. He agreed to do the service at the exact time of the funeral service in the States.

I was touched by his offer and agreed to do it. I didn't plan the service; I just gave him as much information about my father as I thought he would need in order to say a few words during the service, although most of it was what was in my own heart and the love I felt for Dad. Then I ordered flowers for the altar and went home to wait for the day.

I had been concerned about my younger son, nine-year-old Brian, since I'd given him the news of his grandfather's death. Although he hadn't had much time to be with Dad, he remembered the few months we had lived at Dad's house when we were evacuated from Africa during the Biafran War. Brian had been just three years old then, but he loved to follow Dad when he went to tend his garden. Dad would pluck some cherry tomatoes, which he gave to Brian, who popped them into his mouth with gusto. I remember how Dad laughed when those tomato seeds squirted out of Brian's mouth.

Brian remembered those times, too. I recalled how he had written a paper about his grandfather the year before for his second-grade school project, when Dad was ill in a nursing home. He had cut out pictures of cherry tomatoes and old men playing with young boys to add to the paper. His teacher was so moved that she called me up to praise Brian for his beautiful A+ tribute to his grandfather.

When the call from my sister in the States brought me the news of Dad's death, I dreaded telling Brian that he would never see his grandfather again. I had expected him to break down and cry, but he said nothing, then asked if he could go out to play. I didn't understand his reaction, or rather "nonreaction," and I guessed that he didn't really understand what had happened. I decided not to elaborate. Maybe it was better that Brian not be totally aware of what had happened.

Bruce, our sixteen-year-old son, was mature enough to understand. His reaction was normal.

In the days that followed, my memories of Dad grew stronger. It was like reliving my whole life again with all the joys and sorrows. It was hard for me to get on with the Christmas preparations.

Then the day of the memorial service came. I made sure that the boys were dressed in their finest suits and we left for the church. We were the only people in the church beside the pastor and his wife and son. It wasn't like a church back home. This small mission congregation met in one room of a building downtown. There was no organ, just a piano, and we sat on metal folding chairs that were brought out each Sunday for the service. The altar was a small table that also was moved into place for the Sunday services. The white chrysanthemums that I'd bought were in two vases on the table.

Mrs. Hoglen began to play the piano softly, familiar hymns I loved. I had not given her a list of my favorite hymns. As Pastor Hoglen began to speak, I put my arm around Brian, who sat rigidly beside me. The pastor talked about my father's life, mentioning things I had related to him a few days before. But he also said other things I don't remember telling him, and they were all true, all fitting for my father's life.

At a break in the service, the pastor's son, Dean, stood up beside his mother at the piano. He began to play his violin. Dean was in our older son, Bruce's, class in school. It meant a lot to Bruce that Dean had missed school to take part in his grandfather's memorial service.

Mrs. Hoglen continued with the hymn, "How Great Thou Art." I looked at my husband. His father had died several years before. We both remembered that that was his father's favorite hymn, which had been sung at his funeral.

As the pastor continued with the service, summarizing the good life of my father, I felt a movement beside me. Brian was crying. Tears trickled down his cheeks; his young shoulders shook as he tried to conceal the sobs inside him. I hugged him close and said, "It's O.K. to cry, Honey." It was as if he had been hiding all his grief inside for days and at last he could let it out. He did understand what had happened. He just didn't know how to deal with it. And that memorial service let him release those pent-up emotions.

As the strains of my favorite hymn, "Precious Lord, Take My Hand," began, I felt that God had taken my hand and was holding tight. I thanked Him for the comfort of His presence during my hour of grief. It had to be God who directed that service. How else could all those special things have occurred to touch every member of my family? It couldn't have been just coincidence. I know it was God's presence. ∞

Birthday

CAROLYN CAHILL

I move swiftly along Lafayette Avenue in Brooklyn, watching my step on the uneven sidewalk littered with trash and broken glass, while I review my day. I'd worked for most of it, had lunch with friends, and then treated myself to a birthday dinner at a favorite restaurant...*our* favorite restaurant. I'm almost startled when I realize that it's the first time I've thought of Alan practically all day—quite a contrast to my last birthday, the first after his passing, which I spent home alone and mostly in tears.

I realize that it would have been wiser to take the bus, which drops me off in front of my apartment building, instead of the subway, which is seven dimly lit blocks away. During the daylight hours I enjoy my new neighborhood and appreciate the diversity of its people—mostly lower-middle class minority families and young artists. However, after dark, everyone moves inside, locking their doors as the stillness of the night is interrupted by the loud calls and laughter of gangs of young men who come to claim our streets as their turf after dark.

It's early June, and although the temperature and humidity make it feel more like August, I wrap my arms more tightly around myself as I notice the late hour and that I am the only one on the street. Just three more blocks…nothing to worry about.

I smile, remembering how much Alan loved to celebrate both of our birthdays. His excitement prompted weeklong celebrations with little gifts and other gestures leading up to the "big day." *And that song!* I can't believe I hadn't thought of that song today! It was a tradition—we would sing it to each other incessantly, for days, and laugh because we couldn't shake the addictive nature of the tune. The last time I sang the birthday song to him was on his thirty-second birthday, less than a week before he died.

It feels good to remember these things with joy instead of sadness. This birthday truly feels like a new beginning and I am aware that the foot that had been resting in the past is now firmly beneath me, gaining strength to bring me forward into my life.

I see my block ahead, but in my mind I'm in conversation with Alan, telling him about the things I want to create in my life during the coming year, all of which are, in some way, outgrowths of seeds planted during the intense period of time when he was trying so hard to stay alive. I am no longer fully on the Brooklyn street but with him in my mind and heart, feeling the joy of his presence as I silently thank him for the grace we shared during those last months of his life. I feel such love…I feel so joyous.

Loud voices ahead harshly bring me fully back to the darkness of the street and break the rhythm of my pace as I stop in my tracks. There are seven of them, probably in their late teens, wearing baggy jeans. Some of them have on the same red t-shirt, but I don't see what it says. I cannot hear their words, but the sound of their conversation is loud, abrupt, and seemingly arrogant, with no regard for the people whose homes they have stopped in front of.

My heart and breathing have stopped with my feet. I feel threatened, aware of the darkness of the street and that there is no one else within view. If I need help, will any of my neighbors heed my call? My insides start to shake as my mind races. What do I do? I remind myself of the flyers posted around the neighborhood last week, telling of a young woman who had been shot and killed in the middle of the day, just a few blocks from here.

I can't take another route—they've seen me, and if I detour now, what if they follow me? The other streets are darker and more remote than this one. I put my head down and continue walking, a bit faster, and with intent. I will not let them see my fear. I can see the front door of my building just beyond them. *Please God, just let me get to my door.*

With each step I fight off my fear. *I am not afraid.... I will make it home.... They will not harm me.... Please, God, help me through this.* My heart is pounding; I hear it in my ears. *Why so afraid? They are just teenagers. But there are so many of them....*

I see the door to my building just a few doors beyond them. If I can make it there I will be home free. Home. *No problem, there is no problem.* I am almost past them now, and they appear not to notice me, engaged in their own teasing. I walk on, swiftly, wearing a mask of peace and confidence. *Just a few more yards....*

I keep my eyes focused a few feet in front of my steps; my hand is on the keys in my pocket when the young man steps out in front of me.

"Um—excuse me...."

My heart stops. I look up at him. He's about six feet tall, slim, wearing a red football jersey and a blue bandana tied around his head Aunt-Jemima-style. I turn for a second and see that his friends are still involved in their verbal sparring of slang terms that I don't understand, but some of them have stopped, and are watching us with curiosity.

"Excuse me, Miss—"

His voice is not threatening, yet I am afraid. I turn back to him. I open my mouth, but nothing comes out. My heart, which has been contracted in a vice of fear, suddenly begins to soften as this young man in front of me begins to sing.

I stare at him in disbelief as he sings the first line of the song. *Our* song.

I smile. My young man is feeling confident now and starts to sway slightly, with the self-consciousness of the tender adolescent that he is. How could I have feared him? He is so beautiful, my beautiful messenger.

I'm staring at him with wide-eyes and a big grin. I look to see Alan in him, but he does not appear in this boy's eyes, his voice, his smile.... I search his face for even the tiniest spark of knowing of this glorious mystery that has prompted him to sing this song to me tonight. I don't see Alan or that spark, and yet the street seems to light up around us with the birthday song that Alan serenaded me with over and over during the days surrounding the four birthdays I'd spent with him.

He finishes and I remain staring at him, embracing him in the love of my gaze, my mouth open in wonder. I laugh as I ask him, "How did you know that it's my birthday?" With the grace of an athlete but uncertainty of step, he moves away slightly, arms crossing in front of him.

He steps back into self-consciousness, and mumbles "It's a real song, right? They didn't believe it's a real song," pointing to his friends. Although I am astonished that there are people on this planet who do not recognize the Beatles birthday song, I wisely decide to keep that observation to myself. I realize my gaze is making him somewhat uncomfortable and I snap to, turning to his friends and smile "Yes, it is definitely a real song." They barely notice me, as they are back involved in their tangle of jeers and taunts and threats to one another.

I thank him, and walk slowly into my building, and silently give thanks over and over again.

My friend, my love, came back to remind me of the truth—that love crosses between the worlds. How did it work? How did he get that young man to sing to me? I don't know, that doesn't matter. What I do know is that as I reached out to Alan with my thoughts, with joy and love, in doing so I made a space for him to reach back.

A Letter From Heaven

A. A.

The last time I ever saw my best friend I said, "Don't die, okay?"

She burst into laughter. We had recently seen the movie *Beaches*, about two best friends, one of whom dies at the end. The movie had deeply touched us, especially since we saw it together. She thought I was joking.

"I'll do my best to stay alive," my best friend said sarcastically as I got in my car and waved good-bye to her. We had just graduated from high school, and my friend was going to spend her summer working at a resort in New England. After the summer was over, she would be going to college on a scholarship.

During the drive back to my rural home, I thought about my adventurous friend and how she seemed determined to take on the universe. I, on the other hand, couldn't even imagine spending an entire summer hundreds of miles away from home.

Besides, I was engaged to marry my high-school sweetheart in December.

I wrote my friend several long letters that summer, mostly telling her, my maid of honor, about plans for my wedding. She sent me only a couple of postcards, saying little more than "wish you were here."

It was just two weeks before she was supposed to come home that we found out she was dead. One of her duties as a lifeguard involved taking groups of guests out in a boat on the river that ran alongside the resort. She was doing just that when some teenagers in a speedboat raced toward her boat full of tourists. The teenagers swerved to miss hitting her boat at full impact, but they hit it just hard enough to knock my precious friend off balance. She fell out of the boat and hit her head as she sank into the water. She drowned before the stunned passengers from either vessel could rescue her.

The first week after her death, I was so upset I could barely get out of bed in the morning. "She told me she wouldn't die," was all I kept thinking.

My December wedding went ahead as planned. I cried the night before my wedding, remembering my dear friend who should have been my maid of honor.

When I returned from my honeymoon, my mother stopped by my new home to give me a letter that had come for me while I was away. Tears filled my eyes as I read the three-page letter.

In it, my friend apologized for not writing more often. She told me what a wonderful bride she thought I would make, and how happy she was for me. She also told me a secret: "I never told anyone this before," she wrote, "but I'm going to study science at college so I can try to become an astronaut. Wouldn't it be fantastic to see the heavens up close?"

The letter was dated the day before she died. I wiped away my tears and smiled. She had gone to see Heaven!

Although I know receiving the letter so much later than it was mailed may have just been a mistake at the post office, I believe my best friend sent me the best wedding present I could ever have imagined—a letter from a friend far, far away.

From *Dorchester Media*

Not Really Alone

HELEN VAN BOXEL

My husband's marriage proposal was surely one of the most startling ever offered. "Darling, would you mind being a widow before you are fifty?"

The tone of his voice, the anxiety wrinkle in his forehead, forestalled any inclination to take the question lightly. "Do not answer hastily," he continued. "You may be left with young children; you may have a mortgage on a home. I would do the best I could, but sometime between now and the next twenty years you would be left alone."

He would not accept my answer then, but said he would come back in a week. I did not need so long. For me there could be no other love, and in spite of the fact that he was a doctor, I would not believe that he was right in this prediction for himself.

In the weeks preceding our marriage there was so much lighthearted gaiety that the serious, long-range view of our marriage was seemingly forgotten. This happy time set the pace of our life together as we lived each day to the fullest.

Four winters ago, in his forty-eighth year, my husband died. Slowly, with increasing wonderment, I have realized that through the years, he had prepared me for this actuality.

The day we reached home from our honeymoon he had said, "Honey, here's $75. If you pay the gas and electric bills promptly, you'll get a nice discount. I'll forget them so you had better take over."

As time went on, he "forgot" more and more. The car would need gasoline or the tires air. Now I realize that he was educating me in both home and car management.

I know, too, when the taxes are due, and the insurance premiums. I was present whenever an insurance policy was purchased, and by my husband's casual questioning of the agent learned his ideas on what would he best to do with them—especially with his life insurance.

Remembering further, I see why he would not let me forget the secretarial skills I had before marriage. He invented a game—the motive is now clear—in which I would take down part of a radio program in shorthand and then read it back to him. Or he would give me a diet list to type for a patient. So my typing and shorthand did not become total strangers—a brief brush-up course restored my confidence.

And then, because an osteopathic physician must keep long hours, and because we never had the children we hoped for, he asked me to be his receptionist during evening hours. Thus I came to know his patients. That I am not alone in knowing my husband, the physician, and can visit freely with those who appreciate him most, is one of the biggest comforts of all.

Today, I am looking at our home with new eyes. Our kitchen was remodeled because my husband said it was "dating" our house. The shelves are reachable now, even without a man's long arm; the drawers open easily. And where the old pantry was, we now have a complete bathroom. "Because sometime, Sweetheart, we may not want so large a house. Some day," he paced a partition line, "we could make it into a duplex."

I walk through the house and see his love everywhere. Upstairs are new combination storm windows. In the basement an automatic gas furnace has replaced the stoker, and the deep freeze means I don't have to shop in bad weather. All these are paid for. He never bought anything until he had the purchase price.

But all these things represent only the material preparations my husband made for the separation he saw ahead. They alone never could have brought peace and comfort to a broken heart.

What more could a man have done for the woman he loved and had to leave? Soon my thoughts inventoried the heretofore taken-for-granted blessings that became mine through marriage to a man whose motto was: God first, others second, self third.

We had often spoken of Divine purpose and plan and had seen ample evidence of it in our lives. Because of this, neither of us ever questioned God's will. We believed that just as we accept the gift of life, so also we must accept its mysteries—with faith. I can see him today as clearly as I ever did, standing before the open window each morning of his life asking for guidance for that day. And in the evening I can hear his prayer of gratitude for whatever the day had brought.

Have I mentioned that my husband was blind? If I have not it is because it seemed so unimportant to our lives. He lost his sight at twelve, one of the long series of physical defeats to which his progressively deteriorating health condemned him—but a more triumphant spirit never lived. We danced and skated, swam and fished as long as he was able.

His only fear seemed to be lest his handicap give him an advantage over other doctors. He refused all special consideration—indeed the compassion all seemed to come from his side. If his books balanced at his death it was because he never wrote down the names of patients who could not pay, and they were legion. And when his wonderful hands were at work, seeking out pain and illness in others, who could say that this man was anything but whole!

But, unimportant though it seemed then, I think of his blindness often now, wondering if it was not this that gave him his incredible sensitivity to the needs of others. Not being able to see the obvious things, he saw the deeper ones, the hidden fears and hopes that are closest to each of us.

How he appreciated, enjoyed and respected people! It is in remembering this that I find the answer to my hardest problem: loneliness. Has he not shown me that the happy life is the useful life? And that in thinking of others we find ourselves? Loving him, I want to be like him; I want to face life with his courage.

When the struggle seems too great and I weakly falter, I have only to remember his thoughtfulness. This comfort sustains me and I realize I am not really alone. ꝏ

Celebrating Our Dreams

KATHRYN LAY

Every November twenty-third I hug my daughter and think of my friend, Linda. Linda died of cancer on a January morning five years ago, leaving behind four young children and a loving husband; but I'm reminded of her friendship and the part she played in my role as a mother every anniversary of the day our daughter came to live with us.

Linda and I shared many things in friendship: the fact that we introduced her to her husband, our love for God and our husbands—and our infertility. Most of all, we shared the strong desire to become a Mom.

After years of watching our friends and family announce the news of their pregnancies, Linda and I shared the pain, frustration, and desperate prayers for a child of our own. Whenever one of us was hurting, we knew we could call the other and she would understand.

Our homes were quiet at Christmas when others were full of excited and noisy children. We came to a point where neither of us went to church on Mother's Day. Whether anyone else understood or not, I knew that Linda did and did not condemn me for my pain. Hers was just as strong.

But then one day she and Ben invited us for dinner and told us of the news that would change all of our lives. They were going to adopt.

We had, of course, considered the same thing years before, but could not afford the expensive baby adoptions from other countries or traditional adoption agencies. Linda and Ben shared the same inability. Yet here they were, filling out paperwork and finding hope once again.

They had learned from an acquaintance that the cost for adopting through the State was minimal, and that you provided a home for a child in need of rescue, hope, and love.

As they went through parenting classes, home visits, and tons of paperwork to fill out; we watched and prayed with them. Was this the right option for us as well?

In six months, they were the foster parents for two brothers, abandoned and so desperate for a loving, safe, and happy home. Richard and I knew that the boys would have all that and more with Linda and Ben. Soon, the boys were eligible for adoption and Linda became the Mom she'd dreamed of being.

They encouraged us to begin the process and we did. As we went through the often exciting, sometimes nerve-wracking experience, Linda was always there to hold my hand, listen to my concerns and joys, and share her own knowledge to make our time easier.

Ten months later, our nine-month-old daughter was placed in our arms. A year after that, we stood before a judge and she became our daughter not only in our hearts, but in the eyes of the law.

Not long after, Linda and Ben took in two more children—two girls, both with medical disabilities. They became a happy and loving family of six.

Linda and I shared our ups and downs, our fears and thrills as new moms. No one else in our circle of friends truly understood what we'd been through and the total joy we were experiencing. No one else knew the hurt I felt when, after years of waiting for my own baby shower my friends got into a conversation over their babies' delivery and birth. Again, I was left out of the conversation, but Linda just winked at me and listened to my stories of the moment I first saw my little Michelle.

Just two years later, Linda was diagnosed with cancer and all too soon she was gone.

Yet, even throughout her illness, when I would call to see how she was doing, she'd quickly ask me about Michelle and my own life. How was my writing? Would we adopt again? And how much her little ones were growing.

I miss Linda. I can still hear her laughter. But I know that whenever I look at my daughter, whenever we celebrate her arrival into our lives, that Linda is still with us and that she was the instrument God used to make the most important dream of our lives come true. ∞

Clocks Stopping

WENDY

When I was cleaning out Mom's apartment one day I commented to my cousin that there was not a clock anywhere in the house—we had moved out almost everything and the phone had been disconnected. I was concerned because I had to be home at a certain time. My cousin left and I was finishing up a few things. I walked by the spare bedroom and heard a clock ticking very loudly. I went in the room and there was a clock that had definitely been in the room before but I could have sworn it wasn't running or ticking prior to that. I still don't know if it was ticking before that or if it just got louder or what, but I had been in and out of that room a thousand times and never noticed it before. It would have been just like Mom to point out the clock so I wouldn't be late for my son's baseball game that day! This clock has become the primary object associated with my experiences. It runs on a single AA battery.

The clock continued to run. I brought it home in July and put it where it was out of the way, yet I could check on it. I was very curious to see when it would stop. I was pregnant when Mom died and of course I was upset that she would never see her first granddaughter. I wanted to take the clock to the hospital with me to see if anything happened. I did not take it but I have since noticed that the clock/date on my camera stopped working between the first picture ever taken of my daughter minutes after she was born and the second picture we took. The date is on the first picture but not the second (you cannot accidentally turn it off, you have to stick a pen or something into a hole and manually change it). It could not have been bumped. I gave my husband an interrogation, he did not touch the date thing between pictures. Why would he? The picture is interesting too—the baby is all lit up but the surroundings are dark. The next picture is completely normal, lit up in a bright hospital room. I had to fix the date later once I realized it had mysteriously been turned off. I think Mom was letting me know she was there.

Anyway, back to the clock. It ran until sometime past Thanksgiving. I'm not sure exactly when it stopped but sometime in November 2002 it stopped at 8:25 (big hand on the five—little hand on the eight).

We put up our Christmas tree on 15 December and it was horrible. Probably the saddest night of my life. I had some of Mom's Christmas stuff and was going through everything—sad. That night before I went to sleep I asked Mom to please come to me in another dream (yes, I'd had several very interesting dreams, also). I was crying and very upset. I wanted and needed her badly.

The next morning I woke up, no dream. Before my husband left to do some shopping I showed him the clock. I said, "Look, Hon, the clock finally stopped at 8:25." I'm not sure why I decided to show him the clock because it had been stopped for a while, but I did and he saw that it was stopped.

About half an hour later I put my twenty-month-old son down for a nap. He had been up there for a while just talking and talking for a long time (it's common for him to talk and "read" his books for a while before he goes to sleep) but this was a long time. I went to the bottom of the stairs to check on him and I heard him say, "Grandma, funny!" and he started cracking up, laughing. I started getting that tingly feeling I had the day Mom died and something told me to come check the clock. I did and it was ticking again!!

I stood there in my kitchen, looking at the clock, crying. I felt Mom move through me again. She was there to comfort me, I know it. The time never changed but that clock ticked (the second hand moved half a second forward and half a second back) until 2 January 2003. I think Mom was letting me know she was there with me through the holidays.

The clock started ticking again on 1 January 2004 and is still ticking but the time is not changing. I'm waiting to see what, if anything, else happens with that. ꝏ

From *After-Death Communication,* Emma Heathcote-James

A Promise Kept

V. M.

The winter of 1978 seemed to be the worst one Ohio had seen in a century. It was very cold, and several inches of snow covered everything. That was also the year when our young twin daughters decided that the only gift they wanted from Santa for Christmas was a puppy. Their father, never one to deny his little girls anything, patiently explained to them that a puppy would get a better start in the spring. The girls looked out at all the snow and ice and realized that it would be hard to train a young animal to go outdoors. So we all agreed that once the weather warmed up, a puppy would be the newest addition to our family.

We forgot all about getting the puppy, though, because my husband died suddenly of a heart attack on April 4. When our shock and grief wore off a little, my children and I talked about the puppy and occasionally looked in the pet stores, but it only made us feel sad.

Then, a few weeks later, the girls and their older brother went into a pet store to buy some fish food. That's when they saw her—the puppy of their dreams. They ran home and excitedly described her to me. Of course I had to go see her at once. She was beautiful, and I think we all fell in love at first sight. But she was so expensive. I cried when I saw my children's faces as I explained that with new school clothes, books and other bills I didn't see how we could afford a puppy at that time.

I felt awful about it, and spent a sleepless night. The next morning I lingered over a second cup of coffee, feeling very depressed. The telephone rang; it was my neighbor calling. She wanted to know if I still had my husband's golf clubs and, if so, would I like to sell them to her brother-in-law. I told her it was fine with me, and hurried down to the basement to find them.

They arrived a few hours later, and the brother-in-law looked over the golf clubs carefully. He said he'd like to buy them and named a figure. It was the exact price of the puppy we'd seen the day before! I agreed to the sale so quickly that the poor man must have thought I was crazy. I couldn't even tell him how to spell my last name on the check.

We bought our wonderful puppy that evening. I don't know whether we were more excited over our new pet or the mysterious way we'd been able to buy her. Those golf clubs had been sitting in our basement since my husband's death over three years ago. Why someone had offered to buy them on that day, for that amount, is not easy to explain. We like to think it was a loving father's way of keeping a promise made to his daughters. ➰

From *Dorchester Media*

Pen-Pal Angel

JENNY SCHROEDEL

Home at last, school finally over, I just wanted to go up to my room—until I noticed the envelope propped on the bottom of the banister in my parents' hallway. My name was written on the front in a shaky, unfamiliar hand. I read the return address. "Richard Flerlage," I murmured. "Who's that?"

I tore open the envelope and began to read. "Dear Miss Jenny Young, your recent letter in *Life* magazine brought back feelings I had when I was your age nearly sixty years ago."

I'd written to *Life* in response to an article about near-death experiences. "Thank you for taking a bold look at that forbidden word, *death*." I was just sixteen years old. Danny, a seven-year-old boy I'd met through my church youth group, was shot and killed. What was the point of his life ending that way? Death haunted my thoughts.

Maybe that's why I was apprehensive about my

future. Teachers, parents, friends all told me what they thought I should do. And now I got unsolicited input from some man in Cincinnati! But I read on. Mr. Flerlage seemed to understand. He told me about serving in Okinawa during World War II when he wasn't much older than I was. Back then he couldn't imagine getting old. Now, though, he was at peace with dying. "Once I accepted that every life ends," he wrote, "I could start to look forward to a future with God."

I thought about Mr. Flerlage's letter a lot but didn't respond until my birthday. I started with the idea of thanking him for writing. I ended up confiding even more of my fears. "Sometimes I feel like God is throwing puzzle pieces at me," I wrote. "And I'm missing the ones that will really help me."

I told him about my life. I even sent him a eulogy I'd written about Danny. In return, Mr. Flerlage sent me a piece he'd written for his local paper about trapping moles in his garden. "I hesitated to send this article," he wrote, "as I look very mean in the picture. But that's what the photographer wanted." I looked at the fuzzy photo showing a mole's eye view of Mr. Flerlage and laughed.

Mr. Flerlage's letters kept coming, somehow always at the right time. Our lives were so different, yet Mr. Flerlage made me feel like he had his all figured out, and I would figure mine out, too. A good friend died in a car accident and immediately I wrote to my pen pal.

"Youth is impatient for answers," Mr. Flerlage explained. "As a wise man once said, 'A man of thirty and a man of sixty may have the same knowledge, but the man of sixty knows what it means.' Looking back, there are so many things I thought I knew but didn't understand. You'll feel the same way one day."

Will I? I wondered. I stopped writing to him after graduating from high school. I put off college to spend a year as a missionary in the Philippines. At the training session I met a fellow missionary named John. Instantly, I knew he was the man I would marry. We got engaged and planned to attend college together. I wanted to call Mr. Flerlage and tell him. "I'll get to hear his voice for the first time!" I said.

I held my breath and dialed. A woman answered. His wife, Freda. "Can I speak to Mr. Flerlage, please?" I asked. "This is Jenny Young!"

There was a long, heavy pause, then she said, "Oh, Jenny. Dick died."

I clenched the phone till my knuckles went white. *Mr. Flerlage is dead?* I'd been so wrapped up in my life and planning my future, I'd let our friendship lapse. Now everything seemed petty and trivial in the face of his death.

"I'm so sorry," I said. "I was calling to tell him I'm engaged to be married."

"That's wonderful!" Mrs. Flerlage said. "Dick would be so happy for you. He loved you very much. Your letters brought him so much joy."

I said good-bye and hung up. I slipped Mr. Flerlage's last letter out of its envelope and read it again. Each word struck me with pangs of regret at my selfishness. Then I got to the end. "Keep on being happy. Run through lots of grass barefoot, but be careful. We want you to enjoy life as it unfolds, and not be hurt by any of it."

Even though I hurt so much, my tears gave way to brighter days, just as Mr. Flerlage promised. John and I married and have a beautiful daughter. Together we run barefoot in the grass. My pen-pal angel's letters were like special deliveries from God. I learn from them still. ꝏ

Much Obliged, Dear Lord

FULTON OURSLER

Her name was Anna Maria Cecily Sophia Virginia Avalon Thessalonians.

She was born into slavery on the Eastern Shore of Maryland and her earthly master had thought it a great joke to saddle the little brown baby with that ungainly Christening. As a young girl, in the first year of her freedom, Ann helped the doctor the day my mother was born. That was in 1866. Thirty-seven years later she was in the bedroom when I was born; she gave me my first bath, but that was not all she gave me.

I remember her as she sat at the kitchen table in our house; the hard old brown hands folded across her starched wrapper, the glistening black eyes lifted to the whitewashed ceiling, and the husky old whispering voice saying: "Much obliged, dear Lord, for my vittles."

"Ann," I asked, "what is a vittle?"

"It's what I've got to eat and drink—that's vittles."

"But you'd get your vittles whether you thanked the Lord or not."

"Sure. But it makes everything taste better to be thankful. In some people's religion the whole family does it every meal. But not my church—I do it just for myself.

"You know," she said, "it's a funny thing about being thankful—it's a game an old preacher taught me to play. It's looking for things to be thankful for. You don't know how many of them you pass right by, unless you go looking for them.

"Take this morning, for instance. I wake up and I lay there, lazy like, wondering what I got to be thankful for now. And you know what? I can't think of anything. What must the good God think of me, His child, but it's the honest truth—I just can't think of a thing to thank Him for.

"And then, what you think? My daughter, Josie, comes opening the bedroom door and right straight from the kitchen comes the most delicious morning smell that ever tickled my old nose. Coffee! Much obliged, dear Lord, for the coffee and the daughter to have it ready for an old woman when she wakes up. Much obliged, dear Lord, for the smell of it—and for the way it puts ambition even into me. Some people try to tell me coffee is bad, but I've been drinking it for fifty years now and I'm obliged to the dear Lord for every cup I get.

"Now for a while I've got to help Josie with the house work. It's a little hard to find anything to thank God for in housework; your ma will tell you the same thing and so will any other woman. But when I come to the mantelpiece to dust the ornaments, there's the Little Boy Blue. How long you think I've had that little China boy? Since before your mother was born. I was a slave when I got it for Christmas. But I never broke it; never even got it chipped. There he sits, all shiny blue, on the mantel, with his golden horn to his mouth. I love that little boy; he's been with me all the time; he's my little mantelpiece brother. Much obliged, dear Lord, for Little Boy Blue.

"And almost everything I touch with the dust rag reminds me of something I love to remember. Even the pictures that hang on the walls. It's like a visit with my folks, here and yonder. Funny, when you get to my age you've got as many of your folks up there as down here. The pictures look at me and I look at them and I remember so much that's good. I get through my housework before I know what I'm doing, I've been so busy remembering.

"You go downtown and look in the windows. So many pretty things."

"But Ann," I broke in. "You can't buy them. You haven't got enough money."

"I've always had enough money for what I want. I don't want those pretty things. What I want a long velvet gown for, trailing halfway behind? But I think it's pretty and I love to stand there and play dolls. Yes, I do. I play dolls in my mind, and I think of your ma, and your Aunt Dot, and your Cousin Leona, how each of them would look in that dress, and I have a lot of fun at that window. I'm much obliged to the dear Lord for playing in my mind, old as I am; it's a kind of happiness.

"Once I got caught in the rain. My daughter Josie thought I would catch my death. But it was fun for me. I always heard about fancy people's shower baths. Now I had me one and it was wonderful. So many things are wonderful. That cool water dropping on my cheeks was just exactly like a baby's fingers—and I always loved them.

"You know, God just is giving Heaven away to people all day long. I've been to Druid Hill Park and seen the gardens, but you know what? I likes the old bush in your backyard a sight better. One rose will fill your nose with all the sweetness you can stand...."

Now Ann must have told me these things at different times, but they have ranged themselves in my memory as one long, husky whispered monologue. For a long while I forgot that she had ever said them.

It was not until trouble had clamped down on me with a throttlehold and my old ego had been battered. An hour came when I recognized danger in my own sense of despair. I searched my memory as a bankrupt frantically pokes through safety boxes, looking for a morsel of counsel. Ann had been a long time mouldering in her grave, but her rumbling half-whispered tones came back to me, with the game she taught me at the kitchen table of searching out every cause for thankfulness.

I urged myself to play that game.... I was in the subway at the time, vile-smelling and overcrowded—and it happened there was a burst of laughter that, probably because I was seeking it, reminded me that sorrow passes...and I looked about me and marked a young girl's eyes shining with hope for the evening; and again, pride in reading of a batsman's home run bringing a glow to the face of a tired old clerk...and when I went up on the street, clean snow was falling; a church was lighted and its open doorway called to me. I went in. And I knelt. And my heart filled with warmth when I began to count over my many gifts, my many blessings—how much—how over-poweringly much I had to be grateful for.

For work to be done—good work that I could put my heart into—I'm much obliged, dear Lord, for that. For the ability to take care of those who looked to me. For my loved ones, who love me more than I deserve. For friends; so many who had reached out or spoken, or who had mercifully kept silent in my troubles. And for utter strangers, whom I knew now God had sent to me in my trial, miraculously on hand to help…I found the words of thanks tumbling from my lips and heard myself thanking God even for difficulties because they renewed my faith….

There's magic in thanksgiving. You may begin with a cup of coffee, but once you start, the gratefulness swells and the causes multiply. Finally, it seems the more you thank the more you have, and the more you get to be thankful for—and, of course, that's the whole spiritual keystone.

The soul of long-dead Ann was a big soul, big enough to see God everywhere. I shall never be as big a soul as she was, but she taught me. The word came from the dingy street where she lived in East Baltimore, with Josie, her daughter, that Ann was dying. I remember mother drove me there in a cab. I stood by Ann's bedside; she was in deep pain and the hard old hands were knotted together in a desperate clutch. Poor old woman; what had she to be thankful for now?

She opened her eyes and looked at us; her eyes lingered with mine. "Much obliged, dear Lord," she said, "for such fine friends."

She never spoke again—except in my heart. But there she speaks every day. I'm much obliged to God for that. ൦

CHAPTER

2

Unforgettable Devotion

Trust in the Lord with all your heart.
Proverbs 3:5, NIV

The Memorable Doctor Boynton

HOPE B. FRIEDMAN

It took me two days to burn the contents of my father's files.

Wishing to spare my mother, I had emptied the drawers of his papers into cartons and carried them behind the garage where I had made a circular chicken-wire pen for their disposal. I had a promise to keep and no passing breeze must whisk away a single record or bill.

Slowly the flames spread from paper to paper, then shot higher as I continued feeding them into the fire. Though my cheeks turned crimson, I stood stirring the fire with a long pole until nothing but charred embers remained. Then, leaning wearily on the pole, I looked at the blackened earth and thought of the hundreds of patients now loosed from their debts to a gentle general practitioner.

Thus I had kept the promise I had made to Dad during my annual visit home the year before, in the summer of 1961. Mother had sent me to Dad's office to call him for supper. He hadn't heard me enter the cottage beside my parents' home where he had moved his medical equipment when he retired after fifty-five years of practice. So I tiptoed up behind his worn swivel chair, gave him a big hug and kiss and said, "What are you doing, Dad?"

He dropped his pen on the massive roll-top desk and sighed. "I never did this until my nurse died. And I'm just too weary these days to keep up with them." What an understatement! He was far from keeping up, for beneath his pen lay a bill dated May, 1953.

His chair squeaked as he turned and nodded toward the files lining the walls. "There's a good many thousands of dollars owed me among those records," he told me. "I want your promise that you'll burn them all when I am gone. Then no one will owe me anything." Then, as if to himself, he murmured, "Except, I hope, a kindly remembrance."

Now just a week after his funeral, I was home again, keeping my promise. When the job was done, I stepped inside the house, my clothes smelling of smoke, and found Mother resting in Dad's large leather chair by the front window where he used to doze with his yellow, battle-scarred tomcat curled up on his lap.

There are times in grief when remembering aloud with a loved one is a healing salve. I sensed this was one of those times, so I sat down and listened while mother reminisced. Dad's first office was beside a saloon, she said. The year was 1904 and his Uncle Waldo had made furniture for it out of apple boxes.

Those were the days when Dad made his house calls on foot or by horse and buggy over dusty or rain-soaked roads, when he delivered babies in homes, when medicines were limited, vaccines undeveloped.

Mother's chin trembled. "Those years were times of much testing. His first month in practice—I remember it so clearly—your father logged twenty-nine office calls, with sixty-three dollars owed and nothing paid. But in October he collected twelve dollars. With that and produce given us by grateful patients, we managed somehow."

Those memories seemed to spark her courage. She squared her shoulders and her large dark eyes looked steadily into mine. "Your dad's faith was immovable. God had called him to his practice. Many people needed him. That was enough."

Enough? Yes, I suppose it was enough, when Dad's care and caring had brought so much satisfaction from seeing hurts healed and lives restored. But now, with Dad gone, when condolences no longer filled mother's mailbox and the postman brought only magazines, bills and circulars, would it still be enough?

In April of 1973 our family planned a birthday celebration. Mother would be ninety. The local newspaper carried her picture and an article about her and Dad. She received many cards and notes in response to it. Among them was one with an unfamiliar name on the return address. Noting it as I helped Mother with her mail, I asked, "Who is Mrs. Kate Vail?"

"Why, I don't remember anyone by that name." She paused, puzzled. "Read me the letter, dear."

The plain envelope contained a single sheet, and, as I unfolded it, a paper slipped out and zigzagged lightly to the floor. It was a check for $7.50.

Dear Mrs. Boynton:

It was a pleasure to see your picture in our local newspaper and to read of the doctor's and your lives over the many years you have lived in our community. And congratulations on reaching your ninetieth birthday.

In 1925 our daughter's foot was seriously injured. Your husband, who was our family physician, took care of it and it healed beautifully. At that time we were having much financial difficulty and $7.50 of the good doctor's bill was never paid. This has always bothered me because that was not the way we did things.

Please find a check enclosed to cover that amount. And thank you for the doctor's kindness and patience.

May God bestow His choicest blessings on you and your loved ones.

Most sincerely,
Kate Vail

A look of astonishment crossed Mother's face. "This is incredible, simply incredible. Forty-eight years and still she remembered!" she whispered. "It's the loveliest letter I have ever received. Read it once more."

Again I read it. Then Mother tucked it beneath her arm, saying softly, "I can't let it go just yet; I want to keep it with me."

The room was quiet as we wept together. Surely, I mused, Kate Vail's bill was among those I had burned.

And then a realization came to me. Out of all those debts Dad had got what he really wanted—a kindly remembrance. I looked at Mother. She was smiling through her tears, her eyes seeing something very far away. Yes, that payment was still enough—for both of them. ⊂⊃

Keeping Watch

MARY M. ALWARD

The farm in southern Ontario where I grew up was a place of wonder for me. I loved the animals and helping with the chores. Okay, I must admit, I was a tomboy. I always wanted to be in the barn or fields.

Uncle Willy was my Mom's youngest brother. He was only ten years older and we were constant companions. We did the barn chores, repaired farm equipment and worked together in the fields. Wherever Uncle Willy was, I wasn't far away.

As I grew, the bond between us grew stronger. He was always there to teach me new skills, explain things I didn't understand and to support me in all I did. He was more like an older brother than an uncle. I loved him dearly.

When I was in my teens, Uncle Willy moved his family to a farm at Dundalk, Ontario. I was upset that we wouldn't see each other on a daily basis, but after all it was only a two-hour drive. We visited each other often and the bond between us seemed to strengthen.

When I was married in 1966, Uncle Willy came to the wedding. He was one of the first to dance with the bride. As we glided across the floor to the music of Blue Spanish Eyes, he said, "No matter the distance between us, I'll always be here for you."

Being a married, working woman, I didn't have as many opportunities to visit Uncle Willie. Still, when we were together that special bond was very evident.

The morning of August 1, 1967, I awoke with a feeling of dread. While washing dishes, about 10 A.M., I gazed out over our scenic property. Suddenly, a sparrow landed on the window sill, looked me directly in the eye and pecked three times on the glass before darting away.

The feeling of dread increased until I was short of breath and my knees felt as if they would buckle. I knew immediately that the sparrow had brought me news of a death—but whose?

At 4 P.M., the shrill ring of the phone startled me, though I had been waiting for it all day. As I reached for the receiver, I somehow knew that the call would be bad news. I was right. Mom informed me that Uncle Willy had been in an accident early that morning. Time of death was 10:01 A.M.

That night I had trouble sleeping. I was overcome

with grief. I'd drift off, only to awaken. I tossed and turned. How could my precious uncle be gone?

Finally, about 3 A.M., I fell into a deep sleep. I awoke, startled. Someone was in the room. I opened my eyes. Uncle Willy stood at the foot of the bed, surrounded by a soft glow. "No matter the distance between us, I'll always be here for you," he said.

In times of sorrow, financial hardships, spiritual difficulties and mental anguish, Uncle Willy has always been my guardian angel—keeping watch, just as he promised.

Grandma Hita

CYNTHIA BROOKS

When I was nine years old the thought of death petrified me. I could not stand the prospect of anyone close to me being taken away, nor could I face the eternal emptiness that I feared was death. Dead. The very word sent me into panic.

One evening, about a year after the birth of my sister, my father announced that my mom's mother, Grandma Hita, was moving in with us. (I called her Grandma Hita because she always called me *mi jita*—her shortened version of *mi hijita*—"my little child" in Spanish.) Dad explained that Grandma's failing health did not allow her to live alone any longer. My heart raced and I felt dizzy. Grandma Hita was old and might die while she was with us!

But after Grandma moved into the baby's room, everything seemed to be all right. Grandma's presence calmed us all. She shuffled quietly throughout the house and was glad to do laundry, press shirts, start dinner and mend dresses. And every night she sat on the edge of her bed and changed the bandages on her badly ulcerated leg sores.

"How did you get those sores, Grandma?" I asked one night. In her broken English she told me that she had been pregnant most of her childbearing years—twenty-one times! Even though only six of her children had survived, the pregnancies had been hard on her body, and her legs in particular. But she never complained.

I got used to wandering into Grandma's room and talking with her as she mended a blouse or wrote a birthday card to one of her other grandchildren. I loved to lie on her bed and visit with her. She became my closest confidant, and I went to her with many of my problems.

One Saturday morning my mother left me a long list of chores. I was not allowed to go out and play until every job was crossed off the list. "How am I going to do all of this?" I whined.

Grandma Hita spoke softly, "I help you, and little by little, *mi jita,* we get it all done."

I noticed Grandma's lips moving while we worked. "What are you doing, Grandma?" I asked.

"I pray to the Lord, *mi jita,*" she said. "God will help us do our work."

Another day I came running home in tears. I was

eleven; Kathy, another neighborhood girl, had just told me the family I had been baby-sitting for regularly had asked her to baby-sit the next Saturday night. I cried in Grandma's lap as I questioned why the family I loved so much would drop me so abruptly. I tried so hard to be the best baby-sitter ever, bathing the three little boys and reading them bedtime stories. I had thought I was appreciated, but now my heart was broken.

Grandma brushed my hair away from my face and whispered, "Don't worry, *mi jita,* justice wins out in the end. Jesus knows what is in your heart. He take care of everything." But I had a hard time believing her.

The next morning, Dale, the mother of the boys, called and asked me to come over. I walked the block to her house, petulant and hurt. Was she going to tell me Kathy would be their regular baby-sitter? But when we sat down Dale placed a pearl ring in my hand. "This belonged to my mother. Since I have no daughters, I want you to have it. You have become such a part of our family that we want you to know how much we love you." She invited me to attend the mother-daughter banquet with her at her church on Saturday night. So that's why she had asked Kathy to baby-sit! Grandma had been right again.

As the days turned into years Grandma became an integral part of our family, and insisted on helping in every way possible. She mended my sister Helen's cheerleading skirt and stitched my brother Kenny's pants. My baby sister, Mary Anne, often took her nap in Grandma's arms.

One evening as I sat on the edge of her bed, I choked out, "Grandma, I don't ever want you to die."

Instead of recoiling in horror, she laughed out loud. "Oh, *mi jita,* you don't mean that. I am so tired. I looking forward to no more sore legs. I looking forward to seeing Jesus and resting in His arms."

"But I'll miss you so much!" I cried.

"Oh, no, *mi jita,* I'm never going to leave you." I looked into her eyes and could not believe what I saw. She was so old and close to death and yet she was happy to talk about it. She held me tight and continued to chuckle.

I watched Grandma closely and noticed how often she prayed. Not just at church or before bed but almost constantly. I too prayed for the serenity Grandma felt about death.

The weekend of my aunt and uncle's twenty-fifth wedding anniversary approached. Early in the week Grandma went to stay with them in Anaheim to help prepare for the festivities. Mom, Dad, Mary Anne and I traveled to the church on Saturday morning for the anniversary Mass. We waited excitedly until my aunt and uncle finally appeared and walked down the aisle to the wedding march. But as they neared our pew I could see my aunt's face was puffy from crying. As she approached she leaned over to my mother and said, "Mama's just had a stroke. She's in the hospital."

I barely remember the next two days except that there were constant comings and goings to and from the hospital. I wasn't allowed to visit—Grandma wasn't conscious, I was told—and I kept myself busy trying to entertain four-year-old Mary Anne.

A few days later I woke in the morning to see my dad sitting on my bed. "Grandma died just a little while ago," he whispered. I hugged my dad, and as I did, instead of being engulfed by the fear and panic I had always expected and dreaded, I felt a surprising peace and calm. Death had happened. My grandmother, whom I loved intensely, had died. But I knew she was where she wanted to be. That night I slept better than I ever had.

I am grown now and have a child of my own. And there are still times I long to lie on Grandma Hita's lap. I miss her. But when my daughter is overwhelmed by a pile of homework, I tell her "Little by little, *mi jita*." Or when my husband laments injustice at his workplace, I say, "Don't worry, Honey, justice wins out in the end. Jesus knows what's in your heart." I feel again the gentle peace I knew when I nestled in Grandma Hita's lap. And I smile, knowing Grandma is indeed still with me—and we are both resting where we belong. ⊙

A Parting Gift

T. J. BANKS

"I remember my aunt's funeral," Dad said suddenly. "She looked like a little wax doll."

We were visiting old family friends who were more family than friends, and I was puzzled by the odd, remote way he said it as much as by the comment itself. So later, when we were alone, I questioned Mom. "He talks like that when he's not feeling well," she said quietly. Watchfully, for it hadn't been all that many years since his heart attacks.

Dad, I came to understand, did have strong feelings against the viewing of dead bodies. Part of that was due to his upbringing: Jewish funerals do not customarily feature open caskets. But there was more to it than that. My parents' first daughter, Roxann, had died at eight months from an undetermined virus. She'd been sick such a short time—a few days at most—and had then seemingly rallied. But Mom had still felt anxious, so Dad had stayed home from work with them.

One moment, he'd been bending over Roxann's carriage in the living room, playing gently with her; the next, his face had gone completely gray. "She's dead," he'd told my mother, and those words had ushered in a long, bleak time for them.

Years later, shortly before my own birth, they'd lost another baby, Jeffry. He'd been born deformed and with a heart that was too small. In all probability, he had been a Thalidomide baby: my mother had been on an unrecorded medication to keep from miscarrying, and it was the era of Thalidomide and DES. Jeff had lived less than a day: he had never cried, and my parents had never seen him.

For years, Mom's dreams were haunted by a faceless baby. But Dad was always glad—if there was anything to be glad about—that he'd never laid eyes on the little soul in the misshapen body who'd come and left so quickly. It was one less heart-breaking picture for him to carry with him. He loved children, and the sight of Roxann fading flower-like before him was one that he never got over. Ever after, his eyes would soften at the sight of a small girl.

He was a good father, all the kinder and more loving for those losses. He was a man of great heart. Which was ironic because, medically speaking, his was a weak one, badly scarred from those attacks of his. And that great heart was broken open yet again when my brother, Gary—his "third son of a third son of a third son," as Dad used to say proudly—was killed in a car accident out in Idaho. Six years after that crash, shortly before his own death, I heard Dad speak to another man about "my boy" and the accident as though it had just happened the day before.

But my dad did what he always did. He kept going, even when he lost the sight in his right eye to glaucoma. He died when I was twenty-two, a little less than three months shy of my college graduation. One evening, he got up from the sofa, where he'd been taking his usual after-dinner snooze; as he neared the kitchen doorway with the dog gate stretched across it, his leg buckled under him. My brother, Craig—the only other person in the house with us at the time—rushed over to him.

"He didn't see the gate," I heard myself say, even though Dad had lurched to the left, not to the right, the blind side. Craig had already guided Dad back to the sofa. "Squeeze my hand, Dad," he begged, his voice unsteady.

"I'm all right," our father stubbornly insisted.

"Dad," Craig said, his voice breaking slightly, "you're drooling."

Next thing I knew, I was on the phone with our family doctor, and Dad was using what voice he had to yell, "Get away from that phone! I'm all right, I tell ya!" Then I was resting my hand on his forehead, gently slipping the aspirin that Dr. Cannon had directed into his mouth. Out of seemingly nowhere, EMTs, my mother, my brother, Marc, and his wife, and my boyfriend, Tim—whom I would later marry and who thought the world of my father—materialized. Dad, lying on the sofa, his head propped up, looked at the EMT kneeling next to him and said very clearly, "Who are you?"

They were the last words I ever heard him say. He slipped into a coma on his way to the hospital and, despite an operation that night to remove the blood clot from his brain, never came out of it. I went back with the rest of the family the next day, but the sight of him lying in the hospital bed, unable to respond, was too much for me. I did not go back. I simply prayed to be able to let him go when the time came.

That time came six days later, early on a Sunday morning. I didn't go to the hospital with Mom, Marc, and his wife, Janie, but stayed at home with Craig. I would, I told myself, see my father later at the mortuary. Still numb, I went down to the cellar and began puttering around Dad's workbench, poking around in his old cigar boxes and tins.

Out of one tumbled my first published newspaper

reviews and features; out of another spilled black-and-white snapshots of a small determined-looking child with her father's face and hair. I must've been four or five. And I suddenly knew what Dad would've wanted.

I did not see my father again. He'd said good-bye to me in his own way—in death, as in life, giving me simple, sure proof of his love.

Signs of Life

JOSEPH F. STIERHEIM

"Wait a minute, Joe!" I stopped the van in the driveway. Mariellen jumped out, ran to the garden and tugged at an old wrought-iron fence post she'd planted among the flowers. "Imagine how beautiful it will be with a vine wrapped round it," she'd said. I'd wondered why she'd bothered dragging it home from a trash pile in the first place. Now she worked it free and returned to the van, cradling the rusty old thing in her arms. We'd spent the last few days hauling our belongings to our new home, a farmhouse in the country, and I was tired. I didn't want any last-minute baggage.

"You'll see what a difference it will make in the new flower garden," my wife insisted. No point trying to argue with Mariellen when it came to her garden, even one that wasn't yet in the ground. "All right," I grumbled, "but let's get going."

Mariellen stowed the fence post in back, and we

headed for the farm. It wasn't a long drive, about thirty miles. The closer we got, the more anticipation grew in me. For a long time Mariellen and I had been dreaming about moving back to the country we both loved. Our years in the city, raising two boys, had been good ones, but we relished the idea of working the land, eating food we'd grown and witnessing the wonders of nature from a front-row seat.

Three months earlier we had seen the property for the first time. We walked through the ramshackle farmhouse and over much of the land, then climbed to a hilltop and looked down at the house and barn nestled among the trees. The farm had stood for over a hundred years, but it had fallen into disrepair. Still, there was a serene, proud beauty about the place something sheer neglect could never erase. "Oh, Joe," Mariellen said, "let's buy it. Think of what we can make of it together!" Mariellen had always been quicker to see possibility, to imagine what could be. And her enthusiasm was infectious.

We moved in late September, and the wrought-iron fence post went straight to the shed. No time to think of a flower garden now; we had our hands full readying the house for the approaching winter. Our sons pitched in. We stripped wallpaper and plaster and built new partitions; Mariellen painted the rooms. Come spring we cleared a few small fields for planting crops—sweet corn, then field corn and oats. "My flower garden will have to wait," Mariellen decided. "A vegetable garden is next on the list." She made the rows, while I built a chicken house. We bought several hens, a calf and a few pigs. By the following year the farm had come back to life, and we were savoring food from our garden.

"We need a place to relax outdoors after a long day's work," Mariellen proposed one evening as the sun melted into the hills. We drew up the plans at our kitchen table, and over the next few weeks laid a brick patio in back of the house. Mariellen set to work on a flower and herb garden that would surround the patio. "Finally," she said. When she finished mulching, I caught her rooting around in the shed. She came out proudly carrying that old wrought-iron fence post. With a sharp thrust into the soft earth, she gave it a place of honor in her new garden. "You watch," she said. "This will make all the difference."

The brick patio became the hub of our life on the farm. It was the perfect place for talking, relaxing, entertaining friends—for enjoying each other. After a patio dinner one night, Mariellen looked around. "There's only one more thing I'd really like to have," she said. "Roses, the little pink ones."

I knew the kind she meant. "We used to call them old-fashioned roses."

"That's the only thing missing, old-fashioned roses. I'm going to plant some right here in the garden."

Somehow, in our next three years on the farm, Mariellen never got around to it. Then, toward the end of January 1983, there came a warm spell. Mariellen stood on the walkway leading to the house. "Smell the air, Joe! Do you think we'll have an early spring?" She gazed out hopefully over the brown field where the vegetable garden would be planted. "And this year, for sure, I'm going to plant those roses!"

A few days later, on a Saturday night, Mariellen died of a brain aneurysm. We had no warning whatsoever, and the shock hit me so hard I felt numb, as if my life had frozen in place.

When spring came that year, the farm came to life as always. It was only my grief that reminded me I was alive, too. I did my chores without satisfaction. One morning I started the vegetable garden. After a couple hours' work, I stopped and stared at the rich dark earth with its staked rows and the new rows awaiting seed. I missed Mariellen's way of looking at things, of imagining what wasn't yet there—seeing the possibilities in an old wrought-iron fence post, a long-neglected farm, in me. What did anything matter now that she was gone? How could there be a purpose to life when all along death waited? The ground at my feet waited for new seeds. What was the difference if I planted them or not? Nothing lasts. I went back to the house.

Months dragged on. I all but ignored the half-made vegetable garden, and that summer the flower garden grew up in weeds. The boys tried to help out. The patio was unkempt, but I no longer had any use for it. As snow covered over the bricks, I passed the year mark of Mariellen's death. Tend the fields, fix that rotted windowsill in the barn, chop wood for the fireplace—or not. "What's the difference?" I'd say.

Spring found me every bit as listless. I ventured out to the patio one morning, remembering how pleased Mariellen had been at what we'd accomplished with this place in the country. She'd stood right where I was standing and claimed we had everything. Everything except those old-fashioned roses. I laughed at how simple Mariellen could make life seem. If only it could be as simple as that for me now. As simple as old-fashioned roses. I reached down to pull a handful of weeds from the terribly overgrown garden. My finger brushed against the old wrought-iron fence post, and I cleared the ground around it. That's when I saw the plant that grew up through the wrought-iron. Fresh new leaves climbed the post. The plant was definitely not a weed. Were those buds?

That summer the plant bore delicate pink roses, old-fashioned roses, the petals like little wings. There by the old wrought-iron fence post that Mariellen had insisted on bringing from the city—there by the patio, in the center of our life on the farm. In my long months of asking "What's the difference?" I thought I'd been asking the question of myself and that no one had heard me. But I was wrong. God had heard me, and He'd answered. It was almost as if Mariellen herself were insisting, "Find life, Joe, even among weeds. Because life always goes on."

Mariellen had always been quicker to see the possibilities in things, to imagine what could be. Not this time. I saw God's message in those old-fashioned roses. It was the promise of life, eternal life. He had answered my question. He had shown me the difference. ∞

CHAPTER

3

A Smile, A Tear

...as sorrowful, yet always rejoicing...
II Corinthians 6:10, RSV

She Is Still With Me

H. M.

My sister and I were twins and enjoyed doing most things together, especially singing. I was the soprano and her voice was a natural alto, so we were always singing in harmony. Even though we were not good enough to do it professionally, we were called on from time to time to sing duets in church and at school. After we became adults we even sang for some civic functions that appreciated free entertainment.

While driving home from work one night, a drunk driver hit my sister's car and she was killed instantly. I felt as if part of me died that night, and my parents began to worry because I was too numb to even cry.

One evening a few weeks later, when I was wondering how I could go on without my sister, I went for a walk like we used to do. The full moon was so beautiful so I started singing one of our favorites, "Blue Moon."

People passed by and smiled but I barely noticed

them until one woman stopped me and asked, "How do you do that?"

"Do what?" I asked.

"It sounds like you're somehow singing in harmony. How can you do that?"

When I thought about it, I realized that my singing had sounded like the way my sister and I would harmonize together! The woman must have thought I was crazy, because I began to cry and laugh at the same time.

"I can do it because my sister is still with me!" I called to her as I rushed away to get home and call my folks. ➰

From *Dorchester Media*

Loving Laura

BARBARA FLAHERTY

From the moment my second child, Laura, was born sixteen years ago, delivered by emergency C-section, her health was precarious. The doctor told my husband, Mark, and me that Laura had hydrocephalus, a condition in which excessive cerebrospinal fluid accumulates in the skull, causing brain damage. "It's likely she'll be profoundly disabled," the doctor said. "I'm sorry."

The prognosis didn't really sink in until they let me see Laura in the neonatal ICU. The back of her head was so enlarged that even to my untrained eye, it was obvious something was terribly wrong. Yet when I looked into my daughter's dimpled face and touched her tiny hand, an incredible love for her surged through me. *Thank You, God, for giving me this precious baby. I promise to do the very best I can for her with Your help.*

And for all of Laura's life, through the more than thirty surgeries she had to have until she died of complications from pancreatitis, I tried. But despite how deeply I loved her—or maybe because of it, since I wanted so much to do right by her—caring for Laura was a struggle. A struggle that overwhelmed me.

The difficulties began before Laura even came home from the hospital. She underwent surgery to insert a shunt in her brain to drain the fluid. While Laura spent her first five weeks in the hospital, Mark and I found out everything we could about her condition. We learned that hydrocephalic children have varying degrees of physical and mental impairment. Even though the doctor warned us that Laura's disabilities would be on the severe end of the scale, there wasn't any question that we wanted to bring her up at home right along with her older sister, Erin.

Several times each day I went to visit Laura in the ICU. The doctor had told me she might not be capable of nursing, but when I held her close, she nestled trustingly against me, and it seemed as if she just belonged in my arms. I allowed myself to hope that taking care of Laura would come as naturally to me as taking care of her sister had.

I found out how wrong I was after we brought Laura home. At the hospital, we'd learned the daily tasks of managing a baby with hydrocephalus, but it was so different when Mark went to work and I was alone with the girls. Laura cried a lot, a high-pitched cry, and she had trouble keeping milk down. I wore myself out trying to soothe her and keep up with Erin, an energetic toddler.

The one bright spot was that the girls bonded right away. "Laura's brain was hurt when she was born," I explained to Erin, and she treated Laura with a gentleness and understanding nobody would ever have expected from a nineteen-month-old. And Laura—as soon as she heard Erin's voice, she'd break into a smile.

One afternoon I noticed that although Laura turned to me when I sang to her, her eyes weren't focused on my face. The doctor later confirmed that Laura's brain damage had resulted in blindness. "She's so helpless," I worried to Mark, "no baby-sitter will want to take her. My maternity leave's almost over. What are we going to do when I can't be here to watch her?" Both of us knew that quitting my job as a dental hygienist wasn't an option. We desperately needed my income, especially with the bills for Laura's medical care and equipment.

Mark and I confided our troubles to our parents and to people at church and at work. We were put on a prayer list, and Mark's mother volunteered to watch the girls the three days a week I was at my job. Some of Mark's business associates put us in touch with a local organization that provided services for disabled children and their families. We were assigned a caseworker who came to our house every week to train Laura in developing what skills she could and signed her up for physical therapy. I was always on the go, between work and the girls' activities and appointments, but still I prayed, *Lord, am I doing enough for my daughters, especially Laura? She needs so much. Help me provide for her.*

In July 1984, when Laura was nine months old, we took the girls to Iowa to visit my folks. The trip was a disaster. Laura's body couldn't adjust to the heat and humidity, and she kept vomiting. It was a relief to go home again and return to our usual, if exhausting, routine.

Laura never learned to sit up on her own. She couldn't speak. She had to be carried from place to place, either in our arms or in a wheelchair. So much of God's world seemed closed off to my daughter, and I despaired that no matter how I tried, I wasn't opening it up to her.

My parents invited us for another visit the following summer. Laura had been so miserable the last time, not even Erin could make her smile. I didn't want to put Laura through that again, and Mark's mom was ill and couldn't baby-sit. I called the child-services organization for advice.

"Have you considered respite care?" our caseworker asked. "I know a great couple who's experienced with kids with special needs. I'm sure they'd love to look after Laura while you're away."

Leave my daughter in the care of strangers? I recoiled at the thought, but our caseworker told me, "I'm concerned about how much stress you're under." At her urging, I agreed to meet Cathy and Jim Petersen.

The Petersens lived a ten-minute drive across town in a house that seemed as bright and cheerful as they were. In their living room, there was a frail little girl lying in a hospital bed by the window—their foster child, who was terminally ill. Seeing Cathy rearrange her daughter's pillows so that she could feel the sun on her face and watch the birds at the feeder outside, I felt immediately reassured. Maybe Laura could stay here while we're gone.

Laura took to Cathy right from the start. She didn't fuss the way she sometimes did in a new environment, and when we went to pick her up after our trip, I noticed she seemed as comfortable in Cathy's arms as she did in mine. That hurt a little, I admit. But even I couldn't resist Cathy's warmth and openheartedness. "We loved having Laura," she told me. "Call us again anytime."

I couldn't have chosen better people to look after my daughter, and I knew that, really, I hadn't. *God, thank You for bringing us the Petersens.*

After I had my third child, my son, Ryan, in the fall of 1985, for the six weeks I was recovering from my C-section and couldn't lift Laura, the Petersens took care of her. "I know you have a lot going on, with your job and three little ones," Cathy said to me at the end of that stay. "If you ever need someone to take Laura, whether it's for a couple of days or a couple of weeks or even longer, we're here."

I thanked Cathy, but I didn't take her offer seriously. After all, I was Laura's mother. It was my job to look after her. And I kept struggling at it, even as I felt myself being crushed under the weight of my obligations. Laura required so much of me, I worried I wasn't giving Erin and Ryan the attention they deserved. When Erin would ask me to play with her, I could only sigh, "Not now, honey." The worst thing was, she'd nod and tell me, "It's okay, Mom. You're tired."

Mark brought up the idea of hiring someone to help with Laura. He said, "If we stretch our budget, we can do it. I'm becoming very worried about you."

"I'm all right," I insisted testily. "I can handle taking care of my kids." Was Mark implying I wasn't a good mother? I was so confused.

Then came our church picnic the following year at a park by the Missouri River. Laura was having one of her bad days. While Mark took our other kids to the playground, I lifted her from her wheelchair and sat her on my lap. I tried tempting her with her favorite snacks, singing to her. She wouldn't stop crying.

Finally a friend said, "Here, let me take her for a bit." When she did, Laura settled down. I was the one who burst into tears. *I am so sorry,* I cried out to God. *You gave me Laura, and I've failed her…failed both of you. All I want is what's best for my daughter. But what more can I do? Lord, I feel so alone.*

Wiping my eyes, I watched my friend stroll along the riverbank with Laura, and the thought came to me, unbidden, *What if the best thing for Laura is to let someone else take care of her?*

I refused to accept it, but the question would not let go of me. Finally I talked things over with Mark. "You know I'd do anything for Laura," I said. "But give my child up to someone else? What kind of mother would do that? It just doesn't seem right."

"Are things so right the way they are?" he asked. "If we could afford for you to stay home with Laura full-time, they might be. But we can't, so you end up overwhelmed. And that's not good for her or you or anyone in this family."

When we spoke to our caseworker, she said, "Have you considered the Petersens? They take children long-term in foster care, and I know they love Laura."

Laura loved them, too, but it didn't make it easy for me to dial their number. "I've tried to take care of

Laura," I said to Cathy, "but I can't do it. I was hoping you might be able to help." My voice broke.

"Barb, it would be my privilege," Cathy said. "Ever since our daughter passed away, I've felt this emptiness inside. Looking after Laura...you don't know how much it would mean to me."

That was small comfort to me the day we moved Laura into the Petersens' house. After we set up her equipment and put away her clothes, I kept finding excuses so I didn't have to go just yet. I smoothed her Grandma Flaherty's quilt over her new bed and arranged her stuffed animals the way she liked them. Finally I ran out of things to do. "Be good for Cathy and Jim, okay, sweetie?" I said, kissing Laura on the forehead. "I'll be back in a couple of days."

It nearly broke my heart to walk out of her room and then, later, to see the questions in her sister's eyes when I came home without her. "Cathy doesn't have to go to work during the week, so she can be with your sister all day. It's better for Laura," I told Erin, trying to convince myself. "We can go visit her anytime, and she'll come here every weekend."

But the first few times we went to the Petersens' to visit Laura, I could hardly see how she was doing through the tears that flooded my eyes. Invariably I'd come home praying I'd done the right thing. It hurt so much to leave her.

After Laura had been living with the Petersens for a month or so, our caseworker said she'd settled in well enough for us to take her home for the weekend. Erin went with me to pick Laura up. The girls stayed in the sunny living room playing patty-cake while Cathy and I went to Laura's bedroom to pack her bag. "I hope you realize how grateful I am to you," Cathy said.

"I'm the one who should be grateful," I said, thinking Cathy was just trying to make me feel better. "You're wonderful with Laura. She really likes it here."

"I'm glad," Cathy said. Then she cocked her head. "Listen."

Laughter floated down the hall from the living room. "That's what I've been missing so much," Cathy said. I remembered the little girl watching the birds, her face warmed by the sun, the daughter Cathy had lost. "Thank you for sharing your daughter and giving me a chance to feel that joy again."

For the next thirteen years, until the end of her life, Laura remained a part of two households, living with the Petersens during the week and with us on weekends. I am struck with awe and gratitude when I look back on it. Only God could have foreseen that what was best for Laura would turn out to be the best for both families who shared her care—and the joy of loving her. ➰

House on the Hill

GLENNA HELLWIG

My brother, Bennie, was forty-five years old when he was diagnosed with large-cell lung cancer. Doctors predicted he had only a few months to live. I worried about him way out there in West Virginia, so far from me in Ohio, and all his seven brothers and sisters. But Bennie loved his little house on a hill in Foster.

"I'll let you know what I decide, Sis," he said when I tried to convince him to come stay with me. He spent a lot of time sitting on his back porch, thinking or looking down the hill at his church, just listening to the frogs and the crickets and the wind rustling in the apple trees. Bennie claimed that the trees swayed back and forth because they were waving to God. That was Bennie. As always he was finding joy in simple everyday pleasures.

I called him regularly, monitoring the course of the disease. I sent him literature from the Arthur G. James Cancer Hospital and Research Institute, which explained experimental treatment that was available for lung cancer patients. The clinic was right near my house, and although he wouldn't be cured there, the treatment might buy him some extra time. Finally, Bennie gave in. He would go to the clinic as an outpatient.

"We're going to make every minute count," I promised him. Early every morning I made his favorite blueberry pancakes for breakfast, and in the afternoon Mom mixed up big pitchers of iced tea—fresh-brewed and with lots of crushed ice. Bennie liked a tall glass mixed with plenty of sugar. My sister, Carol, spoke with the manager of the local Big Bear. "Now, I don't want to come in here and find you out of banana Popsicles," she said. The manager swore that would never happen. When Bennie got his strength back our brother, Carlos, and Bennie's best fishing buddy, Jimmy, arranged one last fishing trip. They'd fished for bass in rivers all over West Virginia. Sometimes Bennie and I just talked together for hours. "I wish I could catch me a five-pound bass," Bennie always said.

Despite his treatments, the disease continued to ravage his body. When he was no longer able to eat or drink, we had to check him into the clinic. I couldn't stand to see him stuck inside, cut off from everything he loved. Cut off from life, really. What was there to stir the senses in a hospital room? What was there that could possibly be a comfort to Bennie?

"Please, God," I prayed one day at work. "The doctors have done all they could, and there's nothing more we can do for Bennie. So could You please take over?"

That night I pushed open the door to Bennie's room. I walked over and kissed his bald head. His salt-and-pepper hair had fallen out during chemotherapy. I pulled the chair close to his bed and put my purse on the nightstand. There I noticed a little paper cup filled with some kind of lotion. *One of the nurses probably left it,* I thought. *Cancer treatments make your skin so dry.*

Bennie opened his eyes and smiled as I took his hand. "If I could trade places with you right now, little brother, I would," I said.

"You take good care of me, Glenna," Bennie said, reaching for the paper cup. "Everyone has." He dipped his fingers into the shiny pink lotion and rubbed it slowly over his arm.

"What is that?" I asked, sniffing the lotion's sweet fragrance.

"Apples," Bennie answered softly. "A lady came into my room last night, smelling just like that. She smelled so good."

"You mean a nurse?" I asked.

"No," Bennie said. "She wasn't a nurse, but she said she was sent to check on me. I asked her what perfume she was wearing and she gave me some of this lotion." He passed the cup to me and I smoothed some of the silky lotion on my hands. "I love the smell of apples," Bennie sighed. "It reminds me of the trees in my yard."

He was so homesick for his little house on the hill that we arranged to have Bennie flown back to West Virginia. Hard as it was for us to accept, he wanted to spend his remaining days in the place he loved best. My older brother, Dallis, flew out to stay with him, and called to let me know that they were settled in.

"Bennie's all set up with the hospice nurse," he told me. "And it sure is peaceful here. The apple trees are in bloom and you can smell them everywhere! The scent is so strong and sweet, it comes right through the windows into Bennie's house. I had no idea apple trees could smell this way."

What a welcome home for Bennie! And a comfort to me: I knew now that he was where he was supposed to be. Three weeks later my brother passed away. Mom and all seven of us brothers and sisters flew out to West Virginia for the funeral.

Outside the funeral home, my sister counted 310 cars, too many mourners to have fit in Bennie's little church at the foot of the hill. When it was my turn to stand by the coffin, I reached into my purse and pulled out a little bottle of apple lotion I had bought at the drugstore. I rubbed some on my brother's forehead and kissed him good-bye.

Our family led the procession to the cemetery in back of Bennie's church, where he would be buried. The sun shone bright and a light breeze whispered through the trees. I closed my eyes and breathed in the sweet scent. As we gathered round Bennie's resting place, I recalled that angels are said to smell like flowers. Perhaps sometimes they smell like apples, too.

Library Hours

MARGARET MENGE

The reading room of the New York Public Library has an elaborately crafted ceiling with inset paintings of a promising blue sky and pink clouds. I sat far beneath it at a table alone with my books one cold winter Saturday afternoon. *Nothing seems promising to me,* I thought, shivering a little as I read away the last of the dwindling daylight. The library wasn't open on Sunday, and I worked during the week, so I spent every Saturday just like this.

I'd moved to New York City the previous summer, after landing a job as a research assistant at a newsmagazine, even though it meant leaving my graduate program in the Midwest. A falling out with my father made getting away from home seem like a good idea, one more step on the road to independence. As luck would have it, I was able to earn credits toward my journalism degree by helping one of my professors. She needed someone to do extensive research from a book that was part of the humanities collection at the New York Public Library, which meant it could not be checked out. So that's where I sat, poring over a tome on psychic phenomena—ESP, spirits, souls. Not my usual reading.

I was determined to plow through a few more pages of *Phantasms of the Living* before heading home to my apartment. I came to a section documenting cases of what the authors called "death coincidences," when the vision of someone who's just died appears to a loved one or calls his name. The idea didn't seem so far-fetched. God might send a message to comfort the living when a loved one passes on, I thought.

An announcement came over the loudspeaker: "The library will close in fifteen minutes. Please return all materials to the front desk." I packed up my notes, returned the volumes I'd been reading, and walked to the subway. I'd hole up in my Brooklyn apartment for the rest of the weekend. Sunday was just another lonely day for me. Not even the church in my neighborhood felt familiar.

The subway was packed Monday morning as usual. I stood gripping the overhead bar for balance. When the train surfaced on the bridge over the East River, I looked at the Manhattan skyline and tried to feel something, some thrill, some awe. Nothing. My job at the magazine was a solitary one. I did research for my boss, which entailed staring at a computer screen for nine hours. Something had to change. But what?

I got to work and turned on my computer. An e-mail from my father. Great way to start the week, I thought. This was how we communicated; he didn't even have my phone number in Brooklyn. The e-mail told of some family news, and a reminder: "Don't forget to send your grandmother a Christmas card."

I hadn't realized how close the holidays were. And my father was right, I did need to write Grandma. She was ninety-eight and lived in a nursing home in Minnesota, her health precarious. Growing up, I'd missed the opportunity to be close to her. She was a good, strong woman, and I'd never know the secret to her strength. It would be lost to me forever.

That night I went home and wrote a pile of cards. In Grandma's I wrote, "Please know that I think of you often." I signed it and dropped it in the mail the next day at the main post office in Manhattan, near my office. *Please, God, let it reach her on time.*

Christmas Eve a friend from back home came to visit. I talked about my lost opportunity to learn from my grandmother. "She would have taken full advantage of the city," I said. We ate a perfect meal in a restaurant I'd never tried before, even though it was on my block. Snow fell gently outside the window. "You're so lucky to live here," my friend said. "What's stopping you from taking the city by storm?"

On Christmas morning I made a promise to myself: I'd do it. I had the week off from work, and I was determined to make the most of it. I caught up on my sleep, went to the Metropolitan Museum of Art, explored Brooklyn. Three days after Christmas, on Saturday, December 28, I went for a walk around my neighborhood, still blanketed with snow and festive under a bright blue sky. I felt different—lighter, excited, happy. Everything seemed possible. I'd sign up to tutor children, start writing more, invite a coworker to lunch. I was brimming with hope for the New Year. I wanted to remember this day forever. What had caused such a change in me? I wondered.

I jumped out of bed on Monday morning for work. The subway platform was full of bleary-eyed commuters. A woman sloshed a little of her coffee onto my coat in the jostling to board the train.

"Gosh, I'm so sorry!" the woman said, flustered.

"Don't worry," I said. "This coat doesn't show anything." A seat opened up in front of us. "Please take it," I said. "Enjoy your coffee."

The woman smiled, and I did, too. I looked out at the skyline contentedly.

At the office, I sat at my desk and turned on my computer to check my e-mail. A new one from my father. I clicked on it. "Dear Margaret, Your grandmother died on Saturday...."

I sobbed into my hands. People stared. I didn't care. I couldn't stop. I wanted all of it to come out of me, all of the feelings I'd been struggling with since I'd moved here.

Then I looked up again at the e-mail. Saturday, December 28. The day my blues had gone. I thought about my library research project. *God, did you send me a message from Grandma? Was that why I'd had the sudden change of heart?* I thought about it all week. That Saturday at the library, I stared up at those promising pink clouds. Were "death coincidences" the work of angels by another name?

I got my answer in the next e-mail from my father. Right before my grandmother died, he'd opened my Christmas card for her. It arrived late, on December 28. It was the last thing she saw before she died. "Certainly, she was thinking of you," my father wrote.

I'm still in New York, working at the same magazine, but getting some interesting assignments these days. I moved into a better apartment, too, with a shorter commute, and I've made some good friends. Now that I've finished my library research, I spend my Saturdays teaching catechism to fourth-graders at a church near Central Park. I know the ceiling there pretty well, too. It's where I look when I pray. Maybe I'd figured out Grandma's secret after all. ∞

He Came to Say Goodbye

N. M. STACH

When I was fifteen years old my parents moved from the Bronx to a suburb of Rockland County, New York. I was enrolled in the local high school, where I became acquainted with people who later became close friends of mine. One particular boy and I became very close friends and used to speak for hours at a time on the phone or frequently visit each other's homes.

In June of 1967, my friend turned sixteen and applied for a learner's permit to drive. He was going to take his road test during the summer. Unfortunately, he never made it. On July 22, his parents went out for the evening and, since my friend wanted to impress his girl friend, he took his brother's truck for a ride up and down a hill nearby. I was standing on the side of the road with his girl friend as he drove. It had been raining, making the roads slick, and almost inevitably he skidded and crashed. We learned later that he hit his head when he went over a bump in the road, lost consciousness, and the truck went out of control. He died at the hospital from multiple injuries approximately one hour later.

One month after my friend had died, I was lying in my bed when the room suddenly went dark. My bed faced a floodlight outside my window and at first I thought that it had gone out. But when I opened my eyes, I saw my friend standing directly in front of the floodlight. He moved over to me, and when he got right next to me he whispered, "I never had a chance to say good-bye." He bent down and kissed my cheek. Before I even had a chance to say anything to him, he was gone.

I was quite shaken up by this and did not mention it to anyone until about a week later when some friends and I went over to his house to visit with his mother. I decided to tell her what had happened and she asked if I had been able to see what he was wearing. I started to describe his outfit to her—clothes I'd never seen on him before: a blue V-neck sweater, a long-sleeved shirt, beige pants, and cowboy boots. She suddenly turned pale and asked me to go with her for a minute. She took me up to his room, which she had not touched since the day of the accident, and opened his closet. Then it was I who felt faint, for there in his closet was the same outfit I had just described to her!

To this day, many years later, I often think about my friend and I'm happy knowing that he did come back to say good-bye.

From *Dorchester Media*

Up in Her Room

ROB ALARIE

My little sister, Liz, and I were best friends. We both attended Waterloo Oxford High. I was class of 2000; she was one year behind me. We had lots of the same friends and were both big Toronto Raptors fans. Sometimes we'd stay up late at night upstairs in her room, talking—about basketball, crushes, school, movies, life. And, finally, death. You see, Liz had leukemia, and in spring 1998 the doctors told us she wasn't going to make it.

After Liz got too sick even to go to school, those talks in her room became a nightly ritual. Her friends knew how much she liked candles, and she'd been given many as gifts by all the people who loved her. We always lit a few before settling into one of our heart-to-heart conversations. The soft light would illuminate the bright-colored, abstract paintings on her walls, many of which she'd done herself.

"You know, sis, you're not such a bad artist," I said

one night, studying her latest painting. "Even if I have no idea what that's supposed to be."

Liz laughed. Then she caught me completely off-guard. "What do you think's going to happen when I die, Rob?" she asked. Till now my sister and I had talked about everything, except this.

"I don't know, Liz. You'll go to Heaven and it will be a beautiful place."

I wished my answer hadn't sounded so lame. But how could I tell her the truth, that I was scared because I didn't know what to expect? All I really knew was that I didn't want her to die.

"I've had this recurring dream," Liz said, "where I feel peaceful because there are angels all around me. I can feel them, but I can't see them, no matter how hard I try. Kind of like now, Rob. I can feel angels right here in this room. I know they'll take care of me no matter what." I wished so much that I could feel Liz's angels, too.

Liz had a pretty good summer, considering, and even went to see *Titanic*. I found myself hoping she would beat the cancer, despite the doctors' prognosis. But come September, Liz's health took a turn for the worse. She was nauseous most of the time and suffered from constant soreness in her bones. She was soon too weak to leave her bed.

One afternoon early in the school year, Mom

came to pick me up unexpectedly. Liz had slipped into unconsciousness, and her doctor, who had come to the house, didn't think she'd live through the night. I wasn't ready for her to go, but I didn't want her to suffer anymore either.

That evening, I lit Liz's favorite citrus-scented candle and sat next to her on the bed, just the two of us alone. I thought of all the things we'd talked about there in her room—especially about the angels. "I wish I knew for sure that they're with you, sis."

I sensed someone moving behind me and turned to see if one of our parents had come in. No one was there. I looked around at the shadows the candlelight cast upon Liz's walls, the flickering flame playing on her paintings. There was movement in this room. I could feel it. "The angels are here, Liz," I whispered in my little sister's ear. In the candlelight, she looked like an angel herself.

Liz passed away that night, surrounded by those angels she knew from her dreams. I imagined her in Heaven, painting the angels, each and every one, now that she could see them. They had not only come for her that night, they had come for me as well. ꝏ

The Courage Not to Fight

DENISE WICKS-HARRIS

Twilight shadows stole softly across the floor of my new apartment as I nursed my infant son, absorbed in the fresh wonder of motherhood. Long after I finished nursing, I held him close, hearing his tiny breathing, smelling his baby smell. Our small living room turned from mellow to cool dusk. I snapped on the lamp, bathing the room and us in a glow of happiness.

"This is our home, Wilson, cozy and safe," I whispered, kissing his soft cheek. Recently I'd separated from my husband and moved from Philadelphia, Pennsylvania, to Mount Kisco, New York.

At last my life was getting settled. I'd found a job as a domestic where I could keep Wilson with me. Our apartment was in a large complex, convenient to shopping and with wonderful neighbors. There was a big grassy lot and a playground. Important things for Wilson and his older sister, Yolaine, as they grew.

I was still holding this sweet burden of mine when he fell asleep. As I leaned back to rest, suddenly I jumped. A voice, soft and gentle, said, *You will only have Wilson for a short time. Teach him about God.*

My heart was pounding. "Was that You, Lord?" I asked, knowing it was. Shifting a sleeping Wilson to one arm, I went to the window and pulled the cord on the drapes. Would I see an angel? There was only the dark silhouette of the maple tree blowing in the October wind. I hurried to the phone and called my mother.

Her calm, familiar voice reassured me. "Don't worry," she said. "Short time could mean a normal life span because the Bible says, 'A day with the Lord is as a thousand years.' Perhaps God has a special purpose for Wilson and wants you to start teaching him right away."

Of course! I began singing to him and talking to him of Jesus' love.

When Wilson was two he was diagnosed as having hemophilia. It would be hard and often painful for my son, especially since he was so active. But we could live with it.

Then when Wilson was four I got shattering news. Through an infusion of blood protein, he contracted the virus that causes AIDS. The doctor had tears as he told me. I looked this caring man in the eye and said,

"My son will be the one in a million to beat this." The doctor didn't answer, but neither would he dash my hope. We immediately began with the drug AZT, which has prolonged the lives of many AIDS patients.

For five years Wilson continued with his normal routine. Then the virus struck. Still I couldn't believe he would die. I prayed hard.

During the last few months of second grade Wilson began a downslide. He loved school. His teachers were great and wanted him there, despite his physical problems. He was an outgoing child who was popular with all the kids as well.

One day the school nurse called me at my desk where I was a receptionist at Mount Kisco Medical Group. Wilson had had a seizure. He was going down the steps at recess and hit the wall, breaking his glasses. Would I please come right away?

I found him lying on a cot in the nurse's office, his face swollen and bruised. He was dazed but managed a feeble smile and tried to sit up. He was a fighter. I slipped his broken glasses in my purse, knowing they could easily be fixed and wishing all of life was that simple. "Come on, honey," I said, my arm supporting him, "the doctor will adjust your medicine and it will be all right."

And it was. For a little while Wilson was back to his old self, almost. I'd watch him through the bedroom window of our apartment, where kids, just home from school, were gathering. They were skateboarding and after that, chasing one another around the jungle gym. There was a catch in my throat as Wilson drifted to the sidelines and sat lethargically on the grass while Yolaine followed and kept an eye on him. After a while I heard his footsteps, weak and shuffling, on the outside stairs. I opened the door. "Wilson...."

"I'm all right, just tired," he said in his little boy voice that belied man-sized courage. As he reached for a book and slumped on the couch, I wondered if there were any limits to his bravery. There were.

Mid-June came, the last two weeks of school, and Wilson had to drop out. A crushing blow. He was running a high fever that wouldn't break and the doctor had him hospitalized.

Einstein Hospital in New York City's Bronx is an old, plain building fighting its age and looks with fresh paint. Wilson was in the pediatric unit in a small private room with a bed next to a deep-sill window overlooking the street. It had a chair that folded back for me to sleep in at night. I used my vacation and sick time from work to stay with Wilson.

The next day my son was lying weak in bed, having just returned from a bone marrow scan. The doctors still hadn't found the cause of his fever. Fluid from an IV unit was dripping into Wilson's arm. I reached for my worn Bible and opened it to where Jesus gathered the children on His lap. I read to Wilson, picturing those little ones climbing all over Jesus, His strong carpenter's arms holding them protectively and His eyes burning with love. I thought of those hands that healed all who came to Him when He was on earth, and I sent up another prayer.

Then came an ice-cold shock. Wilson looked up at me and said, "I know I'm dying, but I don't want to leave you yet."

I went numb. With all his medical problems—hepatitis, blood transfusions three and four times a week, limbs locking painfully from internal bleeding, seizures—he had never, ever mentioned dying or giving up. Until now. He was a fighter, and it was important that he keep on fighting if he was going to live.

"Honey, you're not dying," I said. "You're sick, but we're going to fight to make you better. You're going to keep on taking your medicine. You'll get out of the hospital and...."

I stopped. His eyes, glued to mine, were pleading. Suddenly I saw the depth of his terror, the awful weight of dying. Of leaving me, his family, friends, his room that meant so much to him, going out of his body and moving to an alien place called Heaven.

Unlike the visits to his uncle in Philadelphia, there would be no phone calls home. Total separation.

I laid the Bible aside and stroked his thin arm. "Jesus loves you, even more than I do," I said. He fell asleep. I sat still in my chair, looking out the window at a lazy summer day. "Jesus," I began, remembering how easily Wilson prayed, about everything small and great, "I can't believe that he's going to die. But if it comes to that, help my son to know that Heaven is wonderful like Your Word says. Help him not to be afraid."

Summer passed in a blur of hospital trips, ups and downs, hope and despair. Before I knew it, the nip of fall had arrived and the leaves were flaming…then withering brown, then gone, and it was winter. Wilson was now bedridden at home.

As the winter wind beat against our building, I tried to think of a way to make Christmas special for Wilson. My mother had moved in with us so I could still go to work. "How about his own tree in his room?" she suggested. We got a table-sized one because his room was tiny. The lights winked at him all through the long nights when he couldn't sleep.

Christmas Day came. Family arrived and we celebrated. Wilson was propped up on pillows on the pullout sofa, his hand resting on one of his presents.

There was a faraway look in his eyes that couldn't be penetrated, not even by the train set we surprised him with, though he managed a smile and ran the train around the track twice. He fell asleep from the effort.

I sank into a chair next to him. From the kitchen came the clatter of pots and pans, and the smells of ham, fried chicken, mashed potatoes and gravy. Wilson opened his eyes and immediately his face searched for mine, as if to confirm that he hadn't left me yet. I finally admitted it. My son was dying.

January 12, a gray, wintry day, I carried Wilson from his bed to the living room sofa. There I bundled him up for this last trip to the hospital. He looked around at each piece of furniture, each picture on the wall, the doorway, the kitchen table and the dishes drying in the sink, soaking himself in memories. "Jesus loves you," I said, praying that Wilson would know it. Really know it.

At the hospital my own strength was about gone, and as day stretched into night I felt strangely numb and detached, almost in shock. Doctors, nurses, family drifted in and out, urging me to sleep, telling me they'd wake me if anything happened—"anything" being the moment of death. The next morning came. Wilson was thirsty, but he couldn't swallow. The soft drink dribbled out of his mouth. As the day progressed he couldn't talk. I remembered a line from his favorite song and could still hear him at church, handsome in his suit, singing for all he was worth: "When I'm sick and can't get well, Lord, remember me.... Do Lord, oh do, Lord, oh do remember me, way beyond the blue."

Please, Jesus.... It was dark again at a quarter to five, and suddenly Wilson became alert, opening his eyes and looking right at me.

"I'm going home, Mom."

How could I explain to him that this was impossible? "Wilson, Mommy can get oxygen for you, but you can't go home with the IV."

"No, Mom. I mean I'm going home to be with Jesus."

Home. He was calling Heaven home. Gone was his dread of leaving me and all else he knew and felt connected to. Wilson's eyes were now focused beyond me. "Jesus is coming to get me. Okay, Mom?"

Jesus Himself coming to take Wilson home. "Yes, Wilson," I said. Fifteen minutes ticked by. My son's eyes closed. His breathing grew more labored. Then stopped. The doctor came in, leaned over and checked his pulse.

"He's gone," the doctor said gently, touching me.

Involuntarily I screamed and grabbed my son by the shoulders. Wilson opened his eyes and started breathing again, a pleading look on his face, as if to say, “Let me go…home.”

In my mind I could see Jesus waiting. “It’s okay, honey. You can go now. Mommy’s all right.”

He smiled, stopped breathing and walked home with Jesus. ∞

CHAPTER
4

The Courage to Try

Then let us no more pass judgment
on one another…
Romans 14:13, RSV

My Abuelita

LUPE RUIZ-FLORES

I was helping my mother in the kitchen that day after school, kneading dough for tortillas. She stood back from the steaming pot of beans she was stirring on the stove, wiped a wisp of moist black hair from her brow and announced matter-of-factly, "You will have to quit school. We will find you a job. There are bills to pay."

I said nothing. My mother had enough burdens already. The meat plant where my father worked had been on strike for nearly a year. He toiled at whatever menial labor he could get. That summer, 1956, our whole family had sweat in the cotton fields under the pitiless Texas sun, praying that by the time we returned to San Antonio the strike would be over. But it dragged on, and I tried to avoid the sadness and worry in my father's eyes as he struggled to provide for us.

Though only fourteen, I felt tired and old. My big sister had married and moved out, leaving me the eldest daughter at home; it was my duty to work and help pay the bills. But I had dreams of being the first in my family to graduate high school.

I loved school, and I also knew an education offered hope of escape from the grinding cycle of poverty that had kept my family down for generations. We dropped out of school to help support our families, married and had children when young, slaved at low-paying jobs and watched the pattern repeat.

But I had a passion for books. The elixirlike odor of musty pages transported me into a world of faraway lands and people whose lives and histories were so different from my own. I hoped someday I would go places I had only read and dreamed about. I knew, though, that without a diploma I was going nowhere.

That day I felt doomed by my mother's pronouncement. What she asked of me was no different from what had been asked of her. She left school in seventh grade to work in a pecan-shelling factory. My father, the son of migrant workers, didn't finish sixth grade. But wasn't there some way of making them understand?

No, my family needed me. Yet I was torn. Why couldn't I just be allowed to get my diploma?

I cried myself to sleep every night, dreading the day when my mother announced they had found work for me. Then something remarkable happened. My grandmother, my abuelita on my father's side, came to visit.

It was not so remarkable that she came, for she

made the difficult trek by bus from Mexico every year to check on the well-being, both spiritual and physical, of her multitude of grandchildren. Quite a sight she was coming up the rutted road, a faded burlap satchel in each hand, one bearing a change of clothes for church and the other bulging with treats for us. She held herself regally. Thick white braids framed her creased brown face, and her full, prismatic skirt, billowing in the breeze, just missed dragging in the dust. A few centuries earlier she might have been Mayan royalty, or so I liked to imagine. Her kisses, coming from such a leathery face, were amazingly soft. She rubbed our feet with her strong hands and told us stories of old Mexico. She helped my mother look after the younger children and at night she shared a bed with the older ones.

As soon as she arrived that first day she quizzed Mother about us. Who was ready for first Communion? Were the older ones studying for confirmation? Here I was trying to resign myself to a life of drudgery and my abuelita was worrying about my eternal soul! It made me more torn than ever about my fate.

Late that night when she thought all of us were asleep, Abuelita stirred. I followed her with my eyes. She rose and stood at the screen door, where a gentle glow from the moon illuminated her face. There was such a softness to her ancient, weathered features, cast in high relief in the silvery light. Even her wrinkles seemed to throw shadows. In her face, as if it were the pages of a library book, I was able to read stories. But these tales were about my family—our struggles, our strength, our faith.

All at once I noticed Abuelita's lips moving. I couldn't make out the words. I saw her in silhouette as she raised her right hand and made the sign of the cross four times; first to the north, then to the east, then to the south, and lastly to the west. There was an indescribable sense of peace in her gestures. When she climbed back into bed I whispered, "What were you doing, Abuelita?"

"Talking to God."

"About what?"

"My children are scattered throughout the world. I ask God to bless them and their children. I talk. He listens. Now go to sleep. It's late."

I couldn't. I knew how to say prayers in church but I had never tried simply talking to God, like Abuelita. But I was desperate. I had never wanted anything more than I wanted to complete high school.

I talked to God until it was almost dawn. I told Him I trusted Him and that whatever course my life took, I would thank Him. I closed my eyes, at peace for the first time in many days.

Not long after, I was taking my usual route home from school when a sign in the dry cleaner's window jumped out at me: Help Wanted. I knew Mr. Ozuna, and rushed in to talk with him, explaining I could schedule work around my classes. He had a daughter my age and was friendly with my family. "I wanted someone here full-time, Lupe, but...okay. When can you start?"

I sprinted home to convince my mother to let me take a part-time job. "Mama, I'll be able to take our clothes to Mr. Ozuna's and have them laundered for free." Mom spent countless hours bent over a wringer-washer. She frowned, knowing how much we needed money. But she also knew how much I wanted my diploma.

A smile crept onto her face, and for an instant I thought I detected a faraway flicker in her eyes, as if she might be remembering some long-abandoned dream. Finally she said, "All right, we'll try it."

I gave her a heartfelt look of appreciation, as close as we ever came to a hug, and said, "Thank you." To myself I said a thank-You to God.

Three years later when I received my high-school diploma, I was the proudest and most grateful young woman in Texas. I am even more so today, knowing my brothers and sisters after me all graduated, too. I had helped break a cycle. I went on to finish college and graduate school and became the first in my family to work in a profession.

When I think back to that time I remember my abuelita, long gone now, walking up our dusty road like a Mayan princess and bringing me the most important lesson I ever learned: When we talk to God, He listens. ∞

The Woman With Golden Hair

ROBERT WILLIAM KELLEY

My journey out of the ordinary world began with another, more commonplace journey—aboard a ship. In the summer of 1998, my wife, Donna, and I decided to leave our kids—Julia, three, and David, six—with my parents and take a short Caribbean cruise. On our first day out, as we walked along the top deck enjoying the view and sea air, a blinding headache dropped me to my knees. Over the course of the afternoon it diminished just enough for me to make it to the musical show we'd planned to see that night. Sitting in the dark, waiting for the curtain to rise, I realized that Donna was weeping beside me.

"What's the matter, honey?" I whispered.

"I don't want you to die," she said.

I felt bad that Donna was so upset, but there wasn't any doubt in my mind that she was overreacting. I was sure the headache would lay off before too long.

But it didn't. Instead, it kept with me for the rest

of the cruise. When we got home, I gave in to Donna's urging and made an appointment with my doctor to put the matter to rest once and for all.

"The headache's probably nothing to be concerned about," he said.

I went home and did as the doctor suggested, forcing myself to take it easy for a couple of days. But the pain wouldn't go away. It got worse and worse, making it impossible even to read or watch TV. *What on earth is happening to me?* After three days without a letup, I went to see another doctor.

An MRI revealed a mass at the center of my brain. Then an angiogram pinpointed the problem: an aneurysm. Surgery would be necessary to correct it.

Days later I arrived at the hospital at 6:00 A.M., after a surprisingly good night's sleep. I can't say why, but for some reason I wasn't all that nervous. I imagined that I would spend a few days at the hospital then go home to Donna and the kids, my strong and self-sufficient self again.

Three hours after Donna watched the orderlies wheel me away, my surgeon came out and informed her that the operation had gone well. "He's in the recovery room. We'll let you know when you can go in and see him."

But after two hours there was still no word. Donna knew something must be wrong.

"Your husband's not coming out of the anesthesia well," a nurse finally explained. The truth was, I was not coming out of it at all.

For over a week, I lay in bed unconscious. Donna sat next to me, praying and watching for the slightest sign of returning consciousness. She fought off fears that she and the kids would never again see me as they knew me—that this lifeless figure, eyes perpetually closed, mouth clamped over a respirator tube, was the last image she would have of her husband.

How could she ever have imagined that the real me was as alive as I'd ever been, right at that very moment?

My adventure began in total darkness, a darkness deeper than any I had ever known. The harder I tried to find my bearings, the blacker it got. I struggled to fight off panic. Then, somewhere out in that vast field of black, a light appeared. I felt immediately drawn toward it. The closer I got, the more my confusion and fear diminished. It seemed I was walking through a tunnel of some kind, with the light at the very end. A breeze was blowing at my back, warm and soothing, like something from a forgotten summer afternoon. It also gently urged me along.

The light grew brighter and brighter, gradually pushing the darkness away. When I felt I was as close as I should be, I stopped. I realized someone else was standing with me, looking at the light, too. I felt, rather than saw, that it was a young boy.

"Uncle Rov, what are you doing here?"

Uncle Rov.... Where had I heard my name said like that? Of course! My nephew, Edward. He used to call me that because he could never pronounce "Rob." He had died of leukemia four years ago, when he was only five.

"Edward! Is that you? Are you all right?"

"Yes, Uncle Rov. But why are you here? Aunt Donna and David and Julia need you."

Someone else joined us. I turned and right behind me I saw a woman, young and beautiful, with golden hair that moved gently in the breeze. Her dress was white with flashes of gold where it reflected the light in front of us. I didn't recognize her, but I sensed the woman knew who I was, just as Edward had.

"Good-bye, Uncle Rov." Edward was walking away now, leaving me alone with the mysterious woman. She gave me a smile of total peace and confidence, and I waited for her to say something. But she remained silent, just standing there and smiling that mysterious smile. Then everything went black again.

The next thing I knew I was back in the ordinary world...or at least above it. I was looking down at a figure in a bed. Me. I was hooked up to a machine that was breathing for me. A nurse was taking readings from the machine. Then the scene changed and in another room I saw Donna, sitting by herself. Tears ran down her face. I could feel her fear and loneliness.

"Don't worry."

The voice came from nearby. Though I couldn't see who was talking, I knew it was that same woman I'd seen before: the woman with the golden hair. She was with me. The scene below changed again. We moved into my son David's bedroom, and I saw him sleeping in his bed. He had his favorite stuffed tiger clutched tightly to him, and was snoring lightly. Then the scene shifted again, and I was in my daughter Julia's room. She, too, was asleep, oblivious to my presence. Her red hair was splayed on her pillow, and her lips moved slightly, as if she were talking to someone in a dream. She had kicked her covers off, and I had an overpowering urge to reach down and tuck them around her again. I wanted to stroke her forehead and let her know that I was fine, that everything was going to be okay. Edward was right. *I don't belong up here yet. Please, God, let me go back to my family!*

The scene changed again, and I was back in my room at the hospital, looking down at myself in bed. The nurse was gone and Donna was beside the bed now, talking to my motionless form. It was so frustrating: There was my wife, heartbroken and bereft, wanting so much to communicate with me, yet completely unaware that I was right there, watching and understanding everything.

I have to return. They need me!

All this time, the woman with golden hair had stayed by my side. I realized she'd been guiding me through these different scenes, taking me from place to place, showing me the people I loved most. Now she spoke again.

"You are right. They do need you. And you will go back to them. But you have to understand it won't be easy. That's why I'm here."

As the woman spoke, the image beneath us changed one more time. The nurse was once again next to me in my hospital room. I could see she was trying to get me to talk. Then she ran out of the room to get one of the doctors. *I'm starting to come back,* I thought.

Then everything went black again. The next thing I knew, I was lying in that hospital bed staring up at Donna's overjoyed face.

Yes, I told the doctors about what I'd experienced. They had another explanation. The woman with golden hair and my meeting with my nephew were hallucinations, they said—the wild fantasies of a brain under stress. I can't blame them for not believing me, but that doesn't mean I don't know in my heart that it happened just the same.

My place is here with my family. They need me, but I need them too, more than I ever did before my illness. My body has new limitations—I'm not as strong as I once was, the threat of a seizure is ever present—and it's crucial for our happiness that I let my family take care of me without getting angry or frustrated about it.

There are moments when it's very hard. I might have to watch Donna tackle some household task that I used to take pleasure in doing for her, or ask Julia to run and bring me a pillow instead of just getting up and fetching it on my own. My weakness can make me feel terrible. After all, I'm supposed to be the provider.

It's at these times that I close my eyes and remember what the woman with golden hair showed me. My place for now is with the living. I'm more limited physically, it's true, but I also know things I didn't before. I know that there's much more to me than just this body of mine, and that the love that binds me to my family has only grown stronger for all my trials. The woman with golden hair gave me that knowledge, and with it in my heart, I can face anything.

The Day I Became a Man

MITKA KALINSKI, AS TOLD TO AMY WONG

If this were the story of someone else's life, I'd know how to begin—with when he was born and how he grew up. About my own birth and childhood, though, there's so little I really know, like who my parents even were, and so much I tried to forget. Only vague impressions, hazy as out-of-focus photographs, remain of my earliest years. People calling me Mitka...a man with a patch over one eye...a woman singing a song about a mother asking her son to come home for dinner...a kind of chant with serious-sounding words that I listened to wearing a small cloth on my head....

This much I know: I was born in the Ukraine sixty-five to seventy years ago. My first clear memories are of the day bombs dropped out of the sky on my boarding school in Bila Tserkva, south of Kiev. It was early summer. I'm not sure how old I was, except too young to know how to read.

I ran as fast and as far as I could, past the edge of town, wandering alone for days, until some men in uniform who spoke a language I didn't understand caught me. The soldiers put me with a bunch of people, and made us drop everything we owned in a pile and walk to the edge of a ditch, the earth freshly dug.

We stood for a long moment. I remember birds chirping. Then the shooting started. The adults standing beside me crumpled, like marionettes whose strings had been cut. I tumbled into the ditch with them. I lay there, my eyes clenched shut, hoping I wouldn't be hit. Finally the chuk-chuk-chuk-chuk-chuk of the machine guns stopped. I opened my eyes. Everything, everyone around me was still. The birds were silent.

The only way out was up. I pulled myself over the lip of the ditch. I got away, but German soldiers recaptured me and put me into a railroad boxcar stuffed with men, women and children. The doors were closed and locked from outside, and the train pulled away. Where were we being taken? The names of the places didn't give anything away. Only too late did we find out that the destination intended for us was a death camp. I am not certain how I escaped that end.

Summer came again. I was transported to a much smaller camp deep in the woods called Pfaffenwald.

Before long, a German officer, Gustav Dorr, took me to work on his family's sprawling farm nearby in Rotenburg on the river Fulda. "Today is December 14, 1942. If you want to live, you will forget everything about your life before this day," he told me. "From now on, your name is Martin Dorr. You speak only German. And your life belongs to me."

There were other prisoners—adults—laboring in the fields, but I was the one Dorr kept at his beck and call. He ran me around the farm from dawn till dark doing chores, the more distasteful the better. Sometimes he ordered me to go through the clothing and posessions he had stolen off internees.

One day I was spreading manure in the fields when I heard something very faintly…music! *Come to me,* the jaunty melody seemed to beckon, like the old song that was all I remembered of my mother. Dorr would whip me if he found out, but I had to follow the sound. Under a tree far from the farmhouse, one of the adult prisoners sat playing a small box-like instrument. "What is that?" I asked.

"This is an accordion," the man said. He slipped the strap over my head, positioned my fingers on the keys and showed me how to use the bellows. I touched a key. Then another. My heart leapt with the notes. As they rose in the air, they also reached deep inside me. I couldn't believe this man had managed to hold on to something so wonderful. "I'll trade it," he offered. "For some speck. A big thick slab."

I knew where the salt pork was kept, and soon the accordion was mine. I hid it in the hayloft, and I would sneak up there and play. I taught myself the songs I overheard the German soldiers singing. I lived for those moments of escape from the grinding misery. So many seasons passed with me forced to labor like a slave, I lost hope that things could ever be different.

One night I crept from my pallet to an open window and stared out at the trees. *Will this ever be over? Will I know anything good in my life again?* In my thoughts, I cried out. But to whom?

Shh…I peered into the night. Was someone out there? No, probably just the leaves rustling in the breeze.

Then it came again, a voice in the darkness, a voice that seemed to come from nowhere and everywhere. *In the end, you will find your goal, what you are looking for. I will lead you.*

A strange energy surged through me, a lightness that somehow made me feel strong. In my arms and legs, my whole body. And deeper, in a place I didn't know the name for.

This strength kept me going all the years I was a captive on the Nazi officer's farm. I didn't even realize the war had ended. Finally, in 1949, United Nations refugee-relief workers rescued me. They called me Dimitri Kalinski. I had not heard my real name in so long it sounded odd to my ears. "Once I was called Mitka," I told the workers.

They took me to a United Nations Refugee Relief Agency village in Bad Aibling, Germany. There was a school, but I was too embarrassed to let on that I didn't know how to read, especially since I was one of the older kids. Besides, I had plenty to learn—how to use a toothbrush and toothpaste, how to eat dinner nicely instead of gobbling like a starving animal, how to get along with other people, not fear and distrust them.

A charity paid my passage to America in 1951, and I couldn't help but recall the mysterious reassurance I heard from the voice that night on Dorr's farm, especially when I saw the magnificent statue standing in New York harbor, the lady holding her torch high. *People come here to start over. That's exactly what I'll do. Start a new life, and never look back.*

I found a job in a factory in Baltimore. One of the guys there nicknamed me Tim. Why not begin my new life with a new name? Weekends I worked on my English. My classroom was the movie theater. Sometimes I watched seven movies in one day, memorizing lines of dialogue so I could practice them later.

Eventually I talked my way into a job as a forklift operator at a factory in North Tonawanda, New York. I didn't know how to drive a forklift. But I figured it out pretty quickly, especially after I saw a girl working in the office who was so lovely she took my breath away. I found out her name—Adrienne—and made sure to drive by her window several times a day. Finally I worked up the nerve to talk to her. One day at the end of our shift, I introduced myself as Tim, then asked, "May I walk you home?" Not an original line, but I'd heard it used with great success many times in movies.

I tried to walk very slowly that evening to make our time together last longer. "You know, I think I've seen you driving the forklift," she said.

"Yes, it's a good job." Our eyes met then, and I felt another kind of music, touching me again in a place deep inside.

I took Adrienne to the movies and to dances and played the accordion for her. About my past I told her only that I had come here from Germany after I lost my parents in the war. She squeezed my hand. "I can guess how hard that must have been. I didn't grow up with my parents, either." Her mother had died young, and she'd been raised by relatives.

Adrienne and I married the same year we met, 1953. I went into construction, and we started our family.

There were better jobs out west, so we moved to Sparks, Nevada, in 1959. I worked hard. It felt wonderful to give our four sons and daughters the carefree childhood I'd never had. To be free. Ours was a good life, one that made it easy for me not to think about the pain of my past. The voice had been right.

Yet I suppose you can never fully escape your past. In 1981, I got hurt in a fall at a job site. I couldn't work. I lost my livelihood, my means of supporting my family, everything. Inside I felt myself collapsing, a terrible dark spiraling feeling. "How can this happen again?" I raged to Adrienne one night. "First Hitler took everything from me. Now this!" The words flew from my mouth before I could stop myself.

"Hitler?" Adrienne stared at me. "Tim, what are you talking about?"

For so long I had kept my secret. Now I told my wife everything. Everything I could remember. Reliving my childhood made me feel like a lost little boy all over again—with no father, no mother, no home, no place where I was loved. I could almost smell the Dorr farm, feel the sting of his strap across the backs of my legs.

"Let me help you," Adrienne pleaded. "We'll put the pieces of your past together so you will be whole."

She began calling me Mitka out of respect for the parents who named me. She talked to the rabbi at a temple in town so I could find out about the faith I'd been born into, and she took me to Friday night services.

The first time I put on a yarmulke, it felt familiar. The prayers began, and a shiver ran up my spine. This wasn't new. I'd worn a yarmulke—at least, a child's version of it—and heard those rich Hebrew words before. Long ago. *You are home,* a voice seemed to whisper.

The rabbi put us in touch with a professor of German, who helped us call Gustav Dorr, still on the farm in Rotenburg. "If I didn't take that little Jewish boy, he would have been gassed," the old Nazi officer claimed. "Had anyone found out, we both would have been killed."

Gary Nixon, a ham-radio operator I met, told me, "I talk to people all over the world. There must be someone out there who knows something about your family." Through his ham-radio connections, Gary found a Colonel Wladyslaw Kalinski in a book of Polish Army officers, and the colonel's daughter, living in England, admitted there had been rumors her father had a son with a Jewish woman. "The only man I remember from when I was little wore an eyepatch," I said.

"My father, he lost an eye and sometimes he had a patch over it!" she exclaimed. In 1997 Adrienne and I went to see my half-sister and to visit my father's grave.

Of my mother, though, there were still no records. That's why it became so important to explore the one connection I had to her: our faith. I learned that a Jewish boy does not truly come of age as a man until he has his bar mitzvah. Could I become a man so late in life?

Last April, Louise Bobrow, who had interviewed me for a Holocaust survivors' foundation, mentioned my story to an Orthodox rabbi in Mineola, New York. Rabbi Anchelle Perl agreed to bar mitzvah me. He called to tell me himself.

"I don't have any official documents proving I have Jewish roots," I said, not wanting to get my hopes up.

"What matters is you have a Jewish soul," the rabbi declared. I couldn't read? He taught me the traditional Hebrew prayers and Torah readings over the phone. "Out of respect for the Almighty, instead of his sacred name, Orthodox Jews use the word Hashem to refer to him," he explained.

On August 20, 2001, I walked into the sanctuary at Rabbi Perl's synagogue, bearing the Torah scroll. I recited the prayers the rabbi had taught me and talked—a little, in English—about what I was feeling after all these years. For so long I had carried this weight around, the weight of my past, of knowing too much and yet not enough. Now I felt such a lightness inside, in the place where I had felt it that long-ago night Hashem spoke to me amid the rustle of the leaves. In my soul.

"Mitka, may Hashem bless you with a life of peace," Rabbi Perl said at the close of the ceremony. "A life of goodness. A life of blessings. A life where your most heartfelt wishes are fulfilled."

How can I look at my life, look at all the people who helped bring me to this place where I feel so loved, and not see that He has indeed? Who else could have transformed the lost little boy Mitka into a man? ➰

Butterfly Lady

BETHANY HOMEYER

Perhaps it was meant to be. For my son's funeral a photo of a monarch butterfly was chosen for the cover of the program. Michael had lost his life at 18 in an auto accident, and in my grief I clung to the hope of that image: the butterfly rising triumphantly from the chrysalis. A symbol of Christ's own promise of life after death.

And yet, in the weeks after the funeral, I found little comfort or reassurance. I dragged myself through daily life—fixing dinner, doing the laundry, driving to the post office—and then sank into despair. The smallest thing would set me off: a vision of Michael running down the path through the garden or stooping to pick a caterpillar off a leaf, each memory a deep ache in my soul.

Michael was my "nature child." He'd bring home insects, presenting them to me as though they were trophies. I'd stand there admiring the ladybugs he held in his chubby hand. "Be careful," he'd say as I leaned close. "Don't hurt them." He might keep them in a shoe box for a day or so, but he always released them back to nature to be free. Once, after washing his overalls, I discovered a bunch of pill bugs in the pockets.

"Look!" I showed the bugs to Michael. "They survived the wash!" We marveled at the hardiness of God's creatures, and let them go in the garden.

Now I kept asking God the impossible: Why couldn't Michael have survived the accident? Why couldn't he bring my son back to me?

The only thing that kept returning to me was the image of that butterfly—a golden monarch fluttering across a clear blue sky, alighting on a flower. In the months after Michael's death I found myself irresistibly drawn to information about butterflies. I read books, looked for courses I could take, spoke with lepidopterists. Was God sending me this passion to fill the hollow space in my heart?

There are tens of thousands of species of butterfly living on every continent of the globe. They fly by day, sleep at night and come in a dazzling variety: The coppery queen lives on milkweed; the black-and-yellow giant swallowtail drinks citrus nectar; the gorgeous ebony-and-yellow mourning cloak feeds on wildflowers. In my studies I felt close to Michael. He would have been fascinated. Sometimes I glanced up from a book and thought he was there, reading over my shoulder. Sometimes I talked to him as if he were still with me.

In time I began to see the study of butterflies not so much as a way to escape my grief, but to embrace it—to honor Michael's memory by doing something he would have loved. *I'll raise butterflies*, I decided.

We had the perfect place, a lakeside garden in our temperate Texas climate. I had always been interested in organic gardening, and we had plenty of trees and shrubs to produce leaves that would feed the caterpillars. I contacted a breeder, bought some larvae and put them in shoe-box-size containers lined with paper towels and leaves. Day by day I watched the caterpillars grow until they formed their chrysalides. Then came the moment when they slowly emerged and unfurled their wings. When they took flight, the sky above my garden was filled with color, as though flowers had taken to the air.

That first summer of raising butterflies brought one joy after another. I felt Michael near me, the way he had been at my side as we watched bees buzz from flower to flower. Released from my sorrow, I wanted to share this beauty with others. I kept thinking about all the milestones that Michael would never reach—graduation from college, his wedding, the birth of his first child. And then I had an idea: Why couldn't I start a business offering butterflies for such occasions? To celebrate beauty, joy and freedom. Michael's Fluttering Wings, I called it. He would have liked that. With the help of some friends, I launched the company.

Since we started Michael's Fluttering Wings five years ago, we have provided thousands of butterflies to fill the gardens and skies at countless events. We take great care of our butterflies, feeding them in their boxes and then keeping them in a large netted cage with plentiful nectar. I am incredibly thankful for this business, the way it lifted me out of my grief and showed me how to move from mourning Michael to honoring him. Yet it was not an overnight process.

Not long ago I was reading about an experiment done by the great English biologist Alfred Russel Wallace. Observing an emperor butterfly struggling to leave its chrysalis, he wondered what would happen if he helped the process along. He slit open the chrysalis with a knife. But, as he wrote, "The butterfly emerged, spread its wings, drooped perceptibly and died." Without the pain and intensity of the struggle to get free, Wallace concluded, the butterfly lacked the strength necessary to survive.

I thought of how I came through the grief of losing my son. It was a long, at times agonizing, struggle, and yet in it I found the strength to go on, to accept the wings God offered. ꝏ

CHAPTER

5

Footsteps to Follow

My steps have held to your paths,
my feet have not slipped.
Psalm 17:5, NIV

I'll Never Forget You, Magic Marge

KATHIE KANIA

Back when I was growing up in New York State, I thought everyone loved my aunt Marge. However, on the way home from my great-uncle Bert's birthday party, when I was nine years old, I found out otherwise.

As I nestled in the back of our old black Chrysler, my head swam with the evening's extravaganza put on by Aunt Marge. There had been a hearty supper of chili, with great slabs of Aunt Marge's homemade bread, glass bowls of her fragrant grape jam, spicy chunks of applesauce, and cucumber relish. We'd all cheered when Great-Uncle Bert blew out the candles on his cake. Then there were games, and, finally, hymns and songs sung in the living room, Aunt Marge accompanying lavishly on the piano, her melodic soprano leading, winding up with all of us singing lustily, "In my heart there rings a melody...."

"Mama, I have an idea," I said in the car. "Why

don't we have another party like that and invite the Millers and…and…."

"Well," Mama began with an uncharacteristic awkwardness, "I don't know about the Millers."

"Oh, Mama," I reassured, "Mrs. Miller would love Aunt Marge!"

"Mrs. Miller knows Aunt Marge," Mama said, picking the words carefully. "She thinks Aunt Marge is…outspoken."

"Outspoken?" I'd never before heard a word against Aunt Marge. "Well, she doesn't know her, Mama, or she'd never say that!"

A parade of Aunt Marge and her activities swam before my eyes: pink-faced from garden work (always with a heaping basket of tomatoes or cukes for us); bare-armed in her clean kitchen, with tiny pearls of perspiration under the stray curl of auburn hair as she kneaded a skin-soft mound of bread dough.

Her darling plumpness gave her lineless face the look of a chubby baby, especially when she laughed, which she often did, and often at herself. "I'm afraid," she'd once announced to a salesgirl as she beheld herself in a frilly blouse, "that I cannot have all this lace marching down my bosom."

We'd dubbed her "Magic Marge" on one of our car trips to visit relatives in Texas. She could locate the sandwich of one's choice with lightning speed from the half-buried picnic basket. She could smooth over unhappy times: When Daddy wouldn't stop for us to go horseback riding, Aunt Marge diverted us with tongue twisters. And when my sister's crayons melted all over Daddy's good hat, Aunt Marge quickly passed out butter toffees and began a rousing chorus of "Way Down Yonder in the Paw Paw Patch" followed by a lengthy discussion as to what a pawpaw might be.

Well, sure, she'd say, "Now, don't put your elbows on the table," and things like that. But outspoken?

As I was entering my teens, I got my first real taste of Aunt Marge's outspokenness. Now that I was incorporated into the all-important caste system of junior high, my birthday celebration had to involve a trip to the shopping plaza. Aunt Marge gladly came along.

"Now, that color..." Aunt Marge said with a certain sigh, "I just hate to say it; I know you like that dress, but that color is not good with your skin."

I trudged stiffly back into the fitting room in the tangerine-colored dress, angrily remembering the "outspoken" charge I'd heard years ago. Then I caught a look at myself in the mirror. Above that dress my skin appeared light blue.

Later, when I was grown up and out on my own, twenty candles were crowded onto the yellow-rose-studded birthday cake Mama and Aunt Marge brought to my apartment in Erie, Pennsylvania. There they inspected my artwork. Portraiture was my first love. I had won an award for a much labored-over portrait of my little sister, Peggy, in her Brownie hat. Aunt Marge's pride in me was embarrassingly wonderful.

"But now, what is this?" she asked, pointing to a young man's portrait by the door. "It's not one of yours."

"Yes, it is."

There was that sigh again. "Kath, it just doesn't seem as good as you usually do."

"Oh, I know," I explained logically, "but he didn't want to pay much."

Silence.

"Do you think," she finally said, "that's reason enough not to do your best?"

I hadn't a leg to stand on. Aunt Marge was right. The portrait did look hurried and superficial.

"Perhaps for less money you could've done a charcoal sketch," she gently suggested, "a really nice one."

Aunt Marge was putting a Kleenex into my hand for the tear on the end of my nose, as she continued, "You know, I learned something many years ago about doing my best. You know how you and your sisters are always exclaiming over my cakes?" I nodded. Aunt Marge transformed herself into Magic Marge every time she took the frosting bag in hand and, with squeezes and calculated turns of the wrist, created the most realistic roses, buds, violets and lacy chains of garlands. We would watch closely and still not know how she did it. "Well, I came close to losing my first job in a bakery," she admitted.

"Why?"

"I couldn't seem to get the hang of it…the little roses…," she sighed. "I don't know if it was an attitude problem or laziness or what. I do know that when I was told about the problem, and faced it, well, I told the Lord—and myself—that I was going to go back in there and do my very, very best." She smiled. "Then things began to happen. Don't let the easy way out ruin things for you, sweetie," she concluded.

Aunt Marge continued to add candles to my cakes until they reached the forest-fire proportions of twenty-six. On Monday afternoons she would call my apartment, and inevitably the conversation would get around to my boyfriend.

"He's just wonderful," I gushed one Monday, speaking of Michael, the guy I'd been going with that summer and fall "What a sense of humor! We like so many of the same things. And he grew up on a farm, too! But…."

"But what?" Aunt Marge asked.

"Well, he's going away to finish his architectural

studies in Europe," I moaned. "He's very travel-oriented and free, and never seems to speak of settling down…you know?" I knew that I didn't have to come right out and explain that I was longing for a home and children. "I told him it might be a good natural break," I said, "a chance to let things die down."

"Is that what you want?"

"No, but if he's not serious…."

"How do you know he's not? Have you told him you love him?"

"Yes," I said. "And he loves me, too. But he's not ready for marriage yet. And I don't want to act pushy."

"Oh," Aunt Marge said, sounding disappointed.

Michael-the-architect flew to Europe that fall, and I pretended that I was healing up just fine. But I felt every tick of the clock.

Then came a surprise phone call—two, in fact—from a young man I'd met while visiting relatives in Texas before I met Michael.

"He is so nice," I bubbled excitedly over the phone. "Oh, Aunt Marge, he wants me to go back to Texas. This is just what I need to get over Michael. Aunt Jane says I can stay with her. It'll be so exciting…."

Below the bright chain of chatter, I was aware that Aunt Marge had remained quiet.

"Aunt Marge, what is the matter?"

I heard that sigh on the other end of the line. "Kath, don't go down there." There was a grave, caring edge to her voice.

"What—what do you mean?"

But now Aunt had transformed herself into Magic Marge again, and this magic I didn't like. "What will happen if you end up with him?" Aunt Marge stated bluntly.

I laughed nervously. "I'm not going to marry him ..."

"Kath, all I know is that the last time we talked you were in love with Michael." She said no more.

Alone in my moonscape of an apartment, I unplugged the phone, I sat in the lavender light of evening without turning on the lamp, and cried and cried. I tried to pray, but all I could think of was *out-spoken, outspoken....* "Outspoken," the portraits I'd labored over seemed to leer. "Outspoken!" That's what Mrs. Miller had said.

But as I prayed I thought about the Lord Jesus—He was sometimes pretty embarrassingly outspoken, too, but always for the benefit of the hearer. For instance, when Martha complained that her sister, Mary, was sitting there listening to His teaching instead of helping her in the kitchen, Jesus' answer was, "'Martha, Martha...you are worried and upset.... Mary has chosen what is better...'" (Luke 10:41,42, NIV). He was outspoken and He never kept silent in the face of someone's wrong decision. He was always turning lives aright.

"Don't let the easy way out ruin things for you, sweetie," I could almost hear Aunt Marge say, and from deep within there was a calm sense of having been pulled to safety from waters that were deep and inviting.

When I turned on the lamp, the first thing I did was call Aunt Marge. Together we picked up the pieces.

Sometimes I look back over the years and wonder how much different things would've been if I'd gone on that trip to Texas. It's impossible to know, of course, and I don't think about it very long. You see, I'm too busy taking care of things and dogs and people I never really dreamed I'd have.

As I tuck my sweet little girls into bed, and Michael and I sip our tea in front of the fire, I thank the Lord in sincerity and amazement for the blessings He had allowed me.

And I thank Him, too, for Aunt Marge. She'll always be Magic Marge to me—but for reasons different from the ones I had when I was nine years old. She taught me never to settle for second best, but to choose the best, do the best, be the best that I can. ꝏ

The Best Is Yet to Come

LISA SMITH

I met Miss Bertha late in her life and only knew her for a few months, but in that time she changed everything for me, freeing me of a fear that had haunted me ever since 1983, while I was in the Marines.

I joined the Corps right out of high school, expecting adventure and travel. What I didn't plan on was falling in love. While stationed at Camp Lejeune, in North Carolina, I met a fellow Marine who'd grown up an hour from my family's country home in Texas. Soon we were talking about rodeos, cattle and schools back home. His name was Dave, and he was sweet, funny, bright and handsome. Within six months we were discussing marriage.

In 1983 Dave was ordered to Beirut for a six-month peacekeeping mission. It was hard to say good-bye, but we both understood that duty came first. And, besides, it wasn't war. It was peacekeeping. We would write every day. And in the spring we would wed.

Then on October 23 I awoke to a news bulletin on my clock radio: "American troops stationed in Beirut were bombed last night as they slept." *No, not Dave!* A building at Beirut Airport that was a temporary barracks for U.S. Marine and Navy troops had been blown up by a terrorist bomber. "Multiple fatalities and injuries are reported," said the announcer, "but no figures can be released until the site is cleared."

I'm sure Dave is fine, I told myself. *He'll call me any minute. Maybe he hadn't even been there last night.*

The phone never rang. Not that day, not the next, as bodies were painstakingly removed from the rubble. I called a friend who worked at division headquarters, hoping to find out more. She received updates every day of the confirmed dead. If Dave's name was on that list, she promised to tell me before I heard from anyone else. For five days I called. For five days I prayed. For five days I barely left the apartment, waiting for news, clinging to a thin strand of hope that somehow the man I loved would be found alive. Then on the sixth day when I called, she burst into tears at the sound of my voice. Dave was gone.

He could only be identified through dental records. I wasn't allowed to see him. There couldn't be any last farewell. I went through his funeral in a daze. I wasn't even his widow, just the woman he was going to marry next year. I felt like a shadow of myself.

Friends assured me life would go on. I would recover. Some years later, I met another Marine named Bob. In time our relationship became romantic, and he asked me to marry him. I loved him dearly, as much as I had loved Dave. I was sure God sent Bob to me. We got married and had two wonderful children. But I couldn't shake the fear that something would happen to Bob, too.

In 1990 he went overseas for Operation Desert Storm and every day I prayed, *Don't let him be killed, God. Don't let him die.* Even when he came home safely after nine months, the fear wouldn't go away. I had grown desperately afraid of death.

Not long after the Gulf War, when we were stationed in Meridian, Mississippi, I found myself rereading an announcement in the paper: "Local Hospice Needs Volunteers." The article quoted one hospice worker as saying, "We need volunteers to give a break to patients' family members." I wanted to help, yet the idea of being so close to death was frightening. Still, something inside me insisted, *I must do this. Lord, give me strength.*

I had several weeks of training and then was assigned my first case—Miss Bertha. She was dying of cancer. On the day I went to see her, I brought some white lilies I had picked. The first thing I noticed was masses of white lilies growing in her flower beds. *Like taking sand to the Sahara,* I thought.

Her husband invited me in and showed me to her bedroom. Miss Bertha was fast asleep in a hospital bed. I leaned over the rail to take a closer look at her. I was about six inches away from her face when suddenly her bright blue eyes popped open. I shrieked.

"Surprise you?" she asked, then burst into raspy laughter. I'd been set up by an old pro.

I hadn't expected to fall for her, but I did, that very day. I loved her smile, her laughter, her sense of fun, and the way she took me under her wing. With her red bandanna covering her head—which was bald from chemotherapy—and her housedress, it was clear that she was the patient, but she never saw it that way. Even that first day she set out to teach me something. Taking the flowers from my hand, she asked, "Do you know how to float lilies?"

"No," I said.

"Let me show you." She climbed out of bed and walked me into the kitchen where she found a glass bowl that I helped her fill with water. Then the two of us snipped off the blossoms and set them adrift in the water. "Don't they look pretty?"

Indeed they did, like sailboats in a bay.

"Now when night comes and the lilies close up, don't you worry, sugar," she told me. "They aren't dead. They're just sleeping. In the morning they'll open up again, pretty as ever."

Twice a week I went to Miss Bertha's. Sometimes I baked corn bread or fixed applesauce for her. I took my Bible with me and read to her. But most of the time we talked. I found out more about her life. It hadn't always been happy. She'd had tough times, financially, and had gone through rocky patches raising four kids. But none of the struggles seemed to get her down. "I just trust the good Lord is watching out for me and that it will all be okay in the end," she said. "He's in charge, not me, so what's the use in worrying?"

One day I told her about Dave and how he had died when he and I were both so young. "It makes me afraid sometimes," I told her. "When Bob went off to Desert Storm, I was terrified that I'd never see him again. I was sure he'd never come back. I'm still afraid...." As I spoke, tears came to my eyes, which embarrassed me because I was supposed to be the one comforting her. I was a Marine.

"God understands, sugar," she said. "You just give Him your fear. He takes good care of us. Then we go to live with Him forever." She hugged me and held me in her frail arms.

Miss Bertha grew weaker. She could barely get out of bed, or even lift her head from the pillow sometimes. I would give her my hand and she'd hold it close to her cheek, just resting.

During our training we had been told that a dying person should be encouraged to talk about death if she wanted. "Are you afraid, Miss Bertha?" I asked one day, and it was as though I were making myself vulnerable to all my own fears.

She shook her head, no. "Honey," she said, her voice just a whisper, "you gotta remember that folks keep on living right up until they die."

"But what about after?"

"Don't you feel sorry for me, sugar. The best is yet to come."

The last time I saw Miss Bertha it was a hot summer day. The fragile white lilies of spring had faded, their place in the flower bed taken by hardy roses and snapdragons. Inside, Miss Bertha's room was cool and dark. Her eyes were closed and her breathing had slowed. I stared over the rail of the bed, almost expecting her blue eyes to pop open as they had that first day, and for her to burst out in laughter.

I thought of Dave, who had been thousands of miles away when his end came. What could I have said to him that might have made any difference? What could I do for Miss Bertha?

I held her hand and touched her face. *No, I won't feel sorry for you because death has come. You're going to live forever.* I had to let go of Dave the same way. There was a better place for Miss Bertha, for Dave, where they would never be far from God's infinite peace and love. "Good-bye, Miss Bertha," I whispered. "Good-bye, Dave. Be at peace."

That night as I looked over at Bob asleep in bed beside me, I felt peace, not fear. When spring came again, I would pick white lilies from the roadside, then take down my best crystal bowl. I'd fill it with water and snip the flowers from the stems, then one by one I'd float them in the water like sailboats. And at night when they closed up their blossoms, I would remember what Miss Bertha told me. In the morning when the darkness ended, they would open up into new life.

Dad's Last Gift

KAREN CHAGNON

It was a struggle for the whole family to watch my father suffer the effects of the bone marrow disease that struck him in his early seventies. It wasn't just the physical pain that got Dad down. It was being prevented from enjoying all the projects and hobbies that had filled his retirement days.

His life had made him an expert at accepting hardship with a courageous attitude. He had spent his entire childhood in foster care. As an adult, nothing gave him more pleasure than seeing kids happy. A talented woodworker, he crafted many a beautiful toy for our children when they were little. When they had all grown up, he took to making dollhouses for the local homeless shelter and church, so that kids from backgrounds like his own could enjoy what he never had.

Dad's other great passion was gardening. Before his illness, he would spend hours tending his flower beds. He had a real green thumb. Plants that got nowhere in my garden came to life in his.

These hobbies of Dad's all came together in a statue of the Blessed Mother that he painted and set up as the centerpiece of his garden. He planted a Rose of Sharon bush on either side of the statue, and over the years they thrived under his care even more than his other plants.

"Dad," I said one day, "I can't believe how those bushes have grown up around the statue."

"Why don't you take home some cuttings for yourself?" he asked.

"Oh, you know me. They won't grow in my garden."

"Give it a try. You might just be surprised."

I found a perfect spot to plant the cuttings, and each summer waited for a lavish burst of blooms. But the summers came and went, and I never got so much as a bud.

"Have my bushes bloomed yet?" Dad would ask. It became our little joke. Still I wished they really would bloom just once.

Then Dad got sick. His health deteriorated rapidly. After several long hospitalizations, he made the decision to spend his last days in the home that meant so much to him.

Dad loved that house the way only someone raised in foster care could. Mom and I set him up in a hospital bed in the living room, so he could have a view onto his beloved garden. The Rose of Sharon bushes had grown so high by that point he could see them without even having to be propped up with pillows.

We worked hard to keep Dad comfortable as his body grew ever weaker, but it wasn't always easy for us to match his courage. Sometimes it got to be too much for me, and I had to go off by myself and pray for strength.

Finally the day came when Dad went to God. He passed from this world just as he had wanted to, at home, surrounded by the people and things he loved.

The day of Dad's wake arrived, and I decided to take a break from preparations. I walked out to the Rose of Sharon bush in my yard, and took a long, close look. Not a single flower had appeared among those leaves in the four years since I had brought the cuttings over from Dad's garden. But as I peered into the foliage, that was just what I saw: a single, perfect bud.

The day after, Dad was laid to rest. And the bud opened into a beautiful flower, a flower that did more to console me in my grief than any words ever could. I took a picture of it, and framed one for each family member so we could see it every day. I think of it as my final present from a man who never stopped giving to others—even after God had called him back into His company. ꝏ

A Ferret Named Polo

APRIL J. MILLER

It was all going to be so perfect. For as long as I could remember, my father had talked about moving to Montana—Big Sky country. We'd taken many a hike amid sun-washed stretches of green grass on our visits there. It was a long way from our home in Georgia, but Dad dreamed of buying a farm in Montana and getting into the burgeoning business of raising ferrets to sell as pets. "Everyone has them out there, April," Dad told me. "They're small and skinny with big raccoon eyes—really frisky and playful. We'll get a place with plenty of room for them to run around." No, it wasn't your standard white-picket-fence-and-a-dog American dream, but it didn't matter. I'd always loved animals, and this sounded like it would be a real hoot.

Dad quit his job and went to Montana to look for a farm. I gave him his first ferret, which he named Jake. "The little guy's a handful," Dad reported on the phone. "He won't let me get into my slippers.

This morning we had a tug-of-war for ten minutes." I laughed, wishing I were already there with him. I gave notice at the executive recruitment firm where I worked, looking forward to trading cubicles and reports for wide-open spaces and frolicking ferrets. Mom and I planned to sell our home and join Dad as soon as he found a place.

But within weeks Dad started suffering severe pain in his hips. When he went to a doctor, he was diagnosed with an advanced stage of cancer. Mom and I rushed to Montana to be with him. Three months later he was dead.

The new life we'd prepared for was over before it had even started. Jake was given away and Mom and I returned to Georgia alone. I couldn't understand why God would choose to take my father right when he was about to live his longtime dream.

Life held no magic after Dad was gone. It was much too painful to talk about, even to God. Mom and I would eat dinner in silence, with no plans for selling our house and running a farm to discuss, no excited phone calls from Dad. I would stop by the pet store sometimes and watch the ferrets scurry around in their pens, imagining my dad wrangling over the slippers with Jake. I could see the bemused smile on his face, hear him telling "the little guy" to let go, and felt the bitter pain of what might have been.

When I went to church, I missed God's presence, too. For the first time in my life I didn't feel that He was with me.

I couldn't go back to my normal routine as if everything were okay. Longing to hold onto some of the thrill of anticipation I'd gotten every time I'd thought of life on a Montana farm, I looked for a job related to animals. A position opened up at a petting zoo and I grabbed the opportunity. At last I'd get the chance to be outside with animals every day the way I would have been on the farm with Dad.

The petting zoo had every kind of animal from llamas to deer to foxes. But, of course, I was drawn to the ferrets. There were two of them, and their antics made them popular with the kids who visited. Still, even though I loved the ferrets, the little creatures were a constant reminder of what I'd lost.

Soon a third ferret arrived. He was particularly small and sable-colored, and his name was Polo. Each time I tried to introduce Polo to the two resident ferrets, they started fighting. "I guess we'll have to find a special place just for you," I said to Polo as I peered into his deep black eyes. "Don't worry, little guy, I'm going to take very good care of you."

I put Polo in a separate pen. He was sickly so I had to take special care to feed him right, and I spent lots of one-on-one time playing with him to keep him from getting too lonely. I felt at ease with him, despite his characteristic ferret hyperness. Taking care of Polo became my reason for getting up in the morning. One afternoon the zoo director told me she thought two ferrets were enough. "Could you find a home for Polo?" she asked. Could I!

That evening I brought Polo home and introduced him to Mom. She reluctantly agreed to let Polo join our household—if he stayed in my room.

My room became the ferret's romping ground. He never sat still. He'd chase me around, then hide behind a piece of furniture before jumping out at me. When I finally collapsed on my bed, exhausted, he'd curl up under my chin and nap with me. One morning I awoke to find him chewing on my slippers. "If only Dad could have seen you," I said to him, remembering Dad talking about the ferret I'd given him. Again the keen pain of loss struck me. I picked up Polo. Stroking his soft fur, I felt a warmth and love that reminded me of Dad. I could almost imagine him reaching down to pet the little ferret, too.

One day when I thought Polo was asleep, I opened my bedroom door. Before I knew it, a furball whizzed by my legs into the hallway. "Mom, look out!" I called. "Polo's on the loose." But he was chasing Mom around the living room. I started chasing Polo, and the three of us ran around the room, Mom shrieking, Polo chucking, and me laughing until we all fell on the couch.

Then Polo hunched his back, leaped into the air and scampered away. Mom giggled. "Guess he's made himself at home," she said.

Mom gave Polo free run of the house after that. He developed a taste for caramel corn, and many an evening he entertained us with his spontaneous games of tag and his aerial acrobatics, which we nicknamed the "weasel war dance." I felt alert again, tuned in—waiting to see what Polo would do next.

After dinner one evening, Mom and I sat watching Polo dash around the house, scattering papers and knocking over knick-knacks. "I don't think your father had any idea what he was getting himself into," she said with a quiet chuckle. I laughed, too. I could picture Dad methodically putting things in Polo's wake back in place over and over.

I came home one evening to find Polo retching. Soon after that he started losing weight and got too sick even to nibble on caramel corn. I could feel every rib in his tiny body when I held him. I took him to the vet for tests. Later that day the vet called back and told me Polo had a tumor. They could remove it, but the operation would cost more than I could possibly pay.

"I can't afford it. I'm sorry. I guess you'll have to put him to sleep," I said, unable to hold back my tears until I hung up.

I didn't go to say good-bye to Polo because I couldn't bear the thought of losing him. Instead,

I went into my room, where I threw myself onto the bed.

When Mom came home and I told her the news, we hugged each other for a long time. It almost felt like I was losing Dad all over again.

I finally managed to get to sleep and was still in bed the next day when the phone rang. It was the vet. He said, "Good afternoon, Miss Miller. Polo made it through the surgery with flying colors."

"What?" I said. "But I thought he was gone."

"One of my technicians fell in love with Polo and wanted to keep him, so she covered the cost of the operation. She says you can visit him anytime."

"Polo's alive," I said quietly. But he wasn't mine. "Thank you, doctor, and thank your technician, too."

I knew I couldn't visit Polo, only to have to go through the heartbreak of leaving him behind. Whether dead or alive, he was still lost to me.

For days I ate little, slept a lot and didn't answer phone calls. One night while lying awake, I could take no more. *God, I miss my father,* I prayed. *I miss Polo. And I miss You.*

I went to church more, desperately seeking comfort. I started, little by little, to talk to others about my father and Polo, to let them pray for me. And I found myself mentioning Dad more in conversations with Mom.

One morning I decided to tidy up the post-Polo

household. Everywhere there were reminders of the lively little creature. Ferret fur all over the sofa cushions, caramel corn stuck in the carpet and his favorite hiding places.

Other memories came back, like Dad saying, "We'll need a big place where they have plenty of room to run around. Just us, the ferrets, and the big Montana sky." I could still see the way his eyes lit up when he talked about it. It wasn't so much the idea as it was his enthusiasm for it that made it special. That, and how much I loved him.

All at once I was overwhelmed with gratefulness to God, not only for the love He had put in my heart for my father, but gratefulness for Polo, who had given me hope that there could be joy in life even after the worst thing in the world had happened.

That afternoon I got a telephone call. It was the vet's assistant who had stepped in to saved Polo's life. "I've gotten a couple of other ferrets now, so if you'd like, you can have Polo," she said. "He's in great shape."

I was on my way to her house in a heartbeat. I picked up Polo and brought him back home. "Now you be careful," I said. "I just cleaned this place up."

With that, Polo scampered across the floor, launched into his weasel war dance and headed for the caramel corn. ∞

Princess Red and the Green Ghost

MARILYN MORGAN HELLEBERG

I have so much to do today, but I can't seem to focus on anything. I try to write a letter, but it ends in mid-sentence. I iron a shirt and reach for another, but standing still is too hard. I give it up. Mechanically, I make the beds, put in a washing and mix up a meat loaf, but nothing holds my attention enough to keep my mind off the news about Jerry. I can't believe he's really dead. Despite his marvelous faith in God, it seems to me that he had more than his share of hardship and tragedy. I'd accepted Jerry's poverty when I knew him as a teenager. I believed God would surely make it up to him one day.

Because I can't seem to do anything else, I climb up on a chair in the basement storage room and dig out the box marked "High School—Marilyn." I blow off the floor and sit cross-legged in front of it. It smells musty, like old books, I open a scrapbook. There's that goofy picture of Jerry and me making faces at the camera, with dandelions stuck all over in our hair and between our teeth.

I smile, remembering how silly we were that day, as we weeded the lawn of the McCook, Nebraska, public library for Miss Slaby in exchange for the use of the Green Ghost (her Model A jalopy). That was also the day Jerry nicknamed me Red, "because of the way the sun dances in your hair." I close my eyes now, and my mind wanders back to those quiet evenings at the library when two shy, bookwormish kids sat on opposite sides of the table, reading Robert and Elizabeth Barrett Browning sonnets to each other in whispers. Before long, we'd discovered that we both loved Thoreau and Emerson, and thunderstorms and rain on the roof, and peanut-butter-and-tomato sandwiches, and writing poetry, and the hush of an empty church. So one winter night, Jerry slipped both of our hands inside his glove and walked me home and we fell in love.

I turn the page and a leaf falls out—thin, flat, brittle. It's from one of those nights when we sat on my porch steps and talked for hours. I think it was the night Jerry told me about his mother and the fish. With ten children, her husband out of work, and no food in the house, Delsie Dike had knelt on the dirt floor of their one-room house and offered her family to God. "You just go ahead and take us all home if You want to, Lord. Or if You're not ready to do that, I know You'll provide." Then, even though it was midwinter, she put on her ragged coat, left with a fishing pole and an ax, and within half an hour she was back with a twelve-pound catfish—enough to feed the whole family for one day.

From then on, Delsie prayed that way every night. And the Lord always provided. Sometimes she'd get a day's work as a cleaning lady, or someone would bring a batch of ironing, or the church ladies would bring in a casserole. Whatever came was usually enough for only one day. "Things are better now," Jerry had said that night on my porch, "but I guess I'm not really sorry for those hand-to-mouth days. We kids learned we could depend on God, absolutely and completely, for each day's needs."

I think it was at that point that the leaf fell onto Jerry's lap and he kissed it and handed it to me. Gently, I place it back in the scrapbook and turn the page.

Poems. Pages and pages of them, in Jerry's handwriting. At the time, I thought they were masterpieces. Now I see that they're not quite as good as they seemed when I had stars in my eyes. And yet, there is Jerry's unmistakable touch.

With the help of a scholarship, Jerry had worked his way through college, graduating cum laude. Just after his illness was diagnosed, I wrote to him, and he sent me excerpts from his fourth unpublished novel. "I've already got a publisher for this one, though! That is, if I'm given the chance to finish it," he'd written. "But if not, that'll be okay, too. Nothing in this world lasts forever, anyway. I'm learning to let go of everything but my faith. And guess what I've discovered, Red? It's all I need!"

I turn more pages, look at pictures of other friends. Here's a piece of crepe paper from the junior banquet, an invitation from Quill & Scroll, my Rainbow Girls pin, some essays from my English class and a confetti streamer. Underneath the streamer I'd written, "Blessed by God, January 1, 1948." It sounds a little silly now. At first I'd been disappointed that Jerry and I weren't going to the New Year's Eve dance. All our friends were buying new formals for the big event, but Jerry couldn't afford the three dollars for tickets, much less a corsage for me. And he didn't have any clothes that would be good enough to wear to a formal dance. I'm ashamed to admit that I blurted out, "Oh, I just wish you weren't so poor!"

Then Jerry said something I didn't understand at all. He said, "There's more to being poor than you think, Red. Maybe you should learn the art." I couldn't figure out what he meant, but by that time I'd learned that Jerry was wise far beyond his years, and he promised me a New Year's Eve I wouldn't forget.

At 5:30 on December 31, 1947, the Green Ghost pulled up in front of our house and out stepped this lovable kid with the rosy cheeks and curly brown hair, in faded jeans and frayed pea coat, topped off with a construction paper top hat and bow tie. Under his arm was a ragged red rug, which he rolled out in front of my door. He bowed low, held my hand high and walked me across the carpet. I didn't know whether to laugh or cry.

The weather was mild, despite the snow that lingered on the ground, and in the Green Ghost we drove to a bank of McCook's Republican River. Jerry had been there earlier, shoveled the snow from a spot under a tree and made a shelter by draping old blankets over its branches. He'd rigged up a table of orange crates covered with oilcloth, and finished things off with a couple of wooden pop cases turned upside down for seats. He helped me out of the car, made a sweeping gesture with his top hat, and said, "Your castle, Princess Red!" So we sat by the river in the middle of winter, eating peanut-butter-and-tomato sandwiches by the light of a pop-bottle candle, and talked about time and eternity, love and God, and those poor dopes dancing around the gym floor in stiff-collared tuxedos and toe-pinching high heels.

About 11:30, Jerry said, "We're going someplace very special to welcome the new year, and he packed up our castle, drove to town and pulled up in front of the little brown church on West First Street. As we got out of the car, we could hear the blare of music from the high-school dance across the street, but as soon as we walked inside and closed the door, a soft feeling of reverence fell over us. Jerry placed our pop-bottle candle on the altar, and we knelt together in the first pew, holding hands and asking God's blessing on the new year. At midnight Jerry kissed me, took two rolls of confetti streamers from his pocket and handed one to me. Then we started chasing each other out of the church, throwing the streamers at each other until we were a tangled mess of colored paper, laughing like hyenas. It sounds a little brazen now, but you know what? I think God loved every minute of it!

I turn the pages quickly now. On the last page is Jerry's Christmas card from the end of that year 1948. Inside, Jerry has written, "If I had the money, I'd give you a diamond tiara and crown you 'Princess Red.' I'm sorry that all I have to give you is this poor card."

My memories of Jerry begin to grow fuzzy as I close the scrapbook and put it back in the box. Sometime during our college years the romance faded, and we realized that, though we were very dear friends—even soulmates—we were no longer in love. I married a few years later; Jerry never did.

I place my memory box back on the shelf now and

get out the letter Jerry sent me after he became ill. A part I hadn't paid much attention to before seems to jump out at me now. "I've resigned my position at F. W. Woolworth and taken a job as a clerk in a clothing store." He went on to say that he'd bought a house for his mother and made provisions for her in the event of his death. That accomplished, he didn't see the point of spending the time left to him "trying to accumulate money (read Proverbs 13:7)!"

Some thought I can't quite grasp flutters just below the surface of my mind as I go upstairs to fix cookies and milk for the children's after-school snack. While they're seated at the counter, eating, I get my Bible and turn to Proverbs 13:7: "One man pretends to be rich, yet has nothing; another pretends to be poor, yet has great wealth" (RSV).

As I clear the counter and send the children outside to play, it occurs to me that I didn't ever adequately answer that 1948 Christmas message from Jerry. If I could do it now, I'd say:

You don't need to apologize, Jerry, for the gift you couldn't afford. The ones you gave me are so much more valuable. When I get discouraged about my work, I think of your four unpublished novels and your refusal to give up. Even your determination was a gift of your poverty, wasn't it? Whenever life seems gray to me, I remember how you always took refuge in your imagination to find a smile, and realize there's one waiting for me, too, in mine. But I think the best gift you gave me was the sure knowledge that the only real wealth is a solid faith. And every year, on December 31, my heart goes back to a makeshift riverside castle and to a little brown church, where I discovered what it means to be poor enough to be truly rich. ൈ

Loving Life Enough

MARY MANACHI

We had just cut the watermelons at a Sunday school picnic and I was laughing at the kids' antics, pretending to play harmonicas as they munched on the sweet pink slices, using the rinds to make big green grins, seeing who could spit seeds the farthest. When I felt the woman's hand on my arm and saw her sympathetic, questioning eyes, I knew what she would say before she even spoke.

"You seem so happy. Really happy. How do you do it after...after all that's happened to you?"

Again and again people ask me that same question—people who know that Louis and I had three children born with the blood disorder called Cooley's anemia. First Mary Lou, then Rosemary, then George. One after the other, they were born with it, lived with it and died of it.

How can I be happy after all that's happened? Well....

Mary Lou was born in 1955. She was our second child, coming two years after our strong and healthy daughter, Ann. At first I had thought Mary Lou's pale skin meant she took after my side of the family. Louis and I are both of Mediterranean descent, but he's the one with the olive complexion. When I took her to the pediatrician for her three-month's checkup, he asked me to set up an appointment for testing. "She seems to be anemic," he told me.

It didn't sound too bad; lots of people have anemia. But after Mary Lou was tested at Cornell Medical Center in New York City, the doctor called Louis and me in for a consultation.

"I'm sorry to have to tell you this," the doctor said. "Your baby has thalassemia major." He explained that this is commonly known as "Cooley's anemia," named after the doctor who identified it. A rare genetic blood disorder, it prevents the body from manufacturing hemoglobin, which carries oxygen from the lungs to body tissues and muscles.

"It mainly affects people of Mediterranean heritage," he told us. He also said that Cornell Medical Center was headquarters for the Harold Weill Clinic, which specializes in treating children with blood diseases. Mary Lou would have to go there every two weeks for a blood transfusion.

From then on I drove my daughter into New York

City from New Jersey regularly. After a few months she seemed to get used to it. And she had company; nineteen other children were being treated there for the same illness.

Louis and I wanted more children, but now we wondered.

"Don't worry," our doctor assured us, "it is rare that this happens in a family twice."

Rosemary was born in 1959. She looked fine—bright-blue eyes and fine brown hair like Mary Lou's. But just to be certain, I took her to the clinic to be examined. The doctors were noncommittal. Weeks went by. One day she would seem perfectly normal, the next her head would be sweating. The pattern had been the same with Mary Lou. Then, when she was six months old, the doctor gently told me that Rosemary would also need regular blood transfusions.

So now I was driving two little girls into the city. It was easy to see how much Mary Lou and Rosemary depended on the transfusions. As the time for the treatment neared, they tired easily and became irritable. But after their hospital visit—grueling as it was—they seemed fine. In the meantime, Louis and I tried to give our three daughters a normal life, with music lessons, Monopoly games and plenty of family outings.

In 1961 our son, George, was born. We had yearned for a boy and we had been assured that the chances of our having another child with the same affliction were nil.

But from the first moment I held my little boy in my arms, I knew. Deep down, I knew. Soon I was taking George into New York along with two-year-old Rosemary and six-year-old Mary Lou.

Even so, Louis and I were grateful for our four lovely children. The blood transfusions simply became a regular part of our lives, and we went on hoping that a medical breakthrough would make them unnecessary. Meanwhile we were busy with the usual family things—school activities and vacations. The years passed. Then came our shocking discovery.

One morning while I was waiting at the hospital, a mother of one of the other children quietly handed me a clipping from *The New York Times* headlined FATAL BLOOD DISORDER. It was about children coming to that very clinic. One sentence blazed out at me: "They usually die before they are twenty years old."

I couldn't believe it. Our doctor had never been that specific. I took the clipping to him. "Is it true?" I asked.

"Yes," he said, sighing. "I'm afraid it is."

There were no drugs, no treatments, no known medical help to prevent my children's death at a young age.

For weeks Louis and I lived in a daze. His reaction

was to say little and concentrate on his work as a garment designer. Mine was to cry whenever I was alone.

The children? We couldn't bring ourselves to discuss it with them, though I knew they were aware of the seriousness of their condition from talking with the other patients during their hospital visits. And then came one of those small moments that can change the way you see things.

I had walked into eleven-year-old Rosemary's room one evening and found her making a jeweled butterfly pin. She was already selling her work at craft shows.

"How beautiful," I said, as I watched her set a rhinestone.

"Thanks, Mom," she said. "I'm going to earn all I can for college."

She was planning on college?

I cleared my throat. "Um…what are you planning to study?"

She looked up, eyes shining. "Nursing, Mom. I want to be like those nice women at the hospital who help me."

She turned back to her work and I walked slowly out of the room, trying to take it all in. Rosemary was not thinking about death; she was focusing on life.

At Thanksgiving one of her teachers phoned me. The class had been asked to write about what they were most thankful for. The answers were the usual ones about home, parents and food. The teacher's voice trembled. "I thought you would like to hear Rosemary's answer: 'I thank God for my good health.'"

Good health? How could she write that? And then I remembered the other children Rosemary saw on her hospital visits, the ones with amputations or suffering from cancer. But Rosemary could walk…go to school…skip rope.

Rosemary had filled our house with Scripture plaques that she made. In her own room she had hung the one that read "This is the day which the Lord has made, let us rejoice and be glad in it" (Psalm 118:24, RSV). That Thanksgiving I looked around me. I saw that our house was not a house of shadows and sorrow; our children filled it with cheerfulness and bustling activity. Mary Lou's piano music rang through the rooms as she practiced for a recital. Rosemary busily made jewelry and plaques. Little George had an extensive rock collection; he was already talking about becoming a geologist. Slowly I began to see that my children, all of them, were rejoicing in life.

On July 4, 1969, Rosemary, then twelve, was in the hospital with a minor cardiac problem, a side effect of Cooley's. "You seem better, Honey," I said as I leaned down to kiss her good-bye. "I'll be back in the morning."

The telephone rang just after I got home. Rosemary was gone. "Peacefully," the nurse said.

Mary Lou and George had known their lives would be short, but with Rosemary gone they were forced to face that fact head-on. Mary Lou, four years older than Rosemary, carefully tended her sister's grave. I knew she must have been contemplating her own death. And yet, I watched as she took up the business of her life with a new vitality. She began making the honor roll in high school and was very popular. And she made a suggestion that gave new direction to our lives.

"Mom," she said, "when I told the kids at the clinic about our vacation to the Poconos, most of them said they had never been to a place like that. Could we find a way to take them with us next time?"

"Of course, we can," I said, hugging her. Suddenly we had a project. I started organizing a volunteer group to take the other children on trips. We held bake sales and candy sales and raised enough money for an excursion to Mount Airy Lodge in the Poconos. Most of the children had never been together outside the hospital. How wonderful it was to see them laughing and having a good time, away from the sting of needles, transfusions and spinal taps. We found ways to raise funds to see a Broadway play and even to visit Disney World.

In 1973 Mary Lou graduated from high school, a member of the National Honor Society. She had undergone surgery to remove her spleen, so she had worked extra hard for those honors. In the fall, she entered William Paterson College as a fine-arts major. Soon she made the dean's list. She worked part-time in a TV repair shop and her civic activities—everything from collecting for charity to volunteer work put her in touch with almost everyone in town.

The following year she volunteered to participate in an experimental drug program for the treatment of Cooley's anemia. It took a lot out of her and she had to be hospitalized for three weeks. "But if it helps other kids, it's worth it," she said.

Mary Lou was nineteen that Christmas of 1974. In January, our Christmas tree was still standing in the living room. For some reason I just couldn't take it down.

On January 20 it snowed heavily, keeping all of us home. Mary Lou practiced her piano in the morning, but got very tired. "I think I'll rest for a while," she said as she went up to bed. Later I brought her some lunch.

"Oh, this soup is so good!" she exclaimed. Then the light suddenly went out of her eyes and she fell back on her pillow.

Mary Lou's funeral was one of the largest ever in West Paterson. Louis and I had no idea she had had so many friends. The mayor and the entire city council were there. In the words of the Cooley's volunteer group member who honored her, she had been "A very special girl who lived and understood life better in her nineteen years than most of us could possibly hope to if we lived to be a hundred."

Later, as a cold rain battered our living room window, I sat alone, thinking about my radiant daughter. Sighing, I leaned back, staring at the wall. In my line of sight were three of the Scripture plaques Rosemary had made: "I will never leave thee, nor forsake thee" (Hebrews 13:5) "Casting all your care upon him; for he careth for you" (1 Peter 5:7) "Do not be anxious about tomorrow" (Matthew 6:34, RSV.) The words blurred in my vision, then cleared. I got up and immediately began preparing dinner for my family.

Our oldest daughter, Ann, was involved in her career, and George, a typical teenager, kept our house lively. His friends came and went and the telephone rang constantly. He dated and had an after-school job at a local restaurant. We continued to take the Cooley's children on trips and have get-togethers.

George graduated from high school and went on to William Paterson, where he threw himself into a full schedule of activities. He continued working part-time at the restaurant, and the summer he was nineteen he bought a sports car—shiny black with fire-engine-red trim. It was a young man's dream and always full of his friends. He kept it in showroom shape.

That's why, on the night of September 20, I knew something was wrong. George came home from a date and after he went to bed I noticed his car had been pulled into the garage at a careless angle. Always before he had aligned it so straight.

The next morning he stayed home from school. "Mom," he said. "I just can't make it. I'm so tired."

Louis and I took him for a long ride that night, knowing the hum and rhythm of the moving car would help him doze off. When we got back to the house, he sank down on the couch. "I know I'm going, Mom," he said wearily. He looked up at me with concern. "Promise me you won't cry? You know where I'll be."

"No, Georgie, I won't cry."

My son smiled, shook his head and lay back, eyes closed. Then he took a deep breath and was gone.

Mary Lou.

Rosemary.

George.

And so, again and again, people ask that question:

"How can you be happy after all that's happened?" I'll tell you how.

My children understood that life is a holy gift from our Creator. They loved each day they were given, and their enjoyment and gratitude were like sunlight, warming and brightening our time together. In the face of early death, they embraced life. If they loved life as much as they did, honoring it, reaching out to soothe their stricken friends, using their days creatively, am I to love life any less?

No! I will not dishonor God—or my children—with gloom and self-pity. I embrace life as they embraced it, and I shall rejoice and be glad in it! ෆ